Copyright 2020 by Harold Schofield -All rights reserved.

No part of this book may be reproduced or transmitted in any form or by any means, electronic or mechanical, including photocopying and recording, or by any information storage and retrieval system, without permission in writing from the publisher. This is a work of fiction. Names, places, characters and incidents are either the product of the author's imagination or are used fictitiously, and any resemblance to any actual persons, living or dead, organizations, events or locales is entirely coincidental. The unauthorized reproduction or distribution of this copyrighted work is ilegal.

Disclaimer Notice:

Please note the information contained within this document is for educational and entertainment purposes only. All effort has been executed to present accurate, up to date, reliable, complete information. No warranties of any kind are declared or implied. Readers acknowledge that the author is not engaged in the rendering of legal, financial, medical, or professional advice. The content within this book has been derived from various sources. Please consult a licensed professional before attempting any techniques outlined in this book.

By reading this document, the reader agrees that under no circumstances is the author responsible for any losses, direct or indirect, that are incurred as a result of the use of the information contained within this document, including, but not limited to, errors, omissions, or inaccuracies.

CONTENTS

Introduction 4
Chapter 1: Intermittent Fasting Explained 6
Chapter 2: Benefits and Downsides of IF 9
Chapter 3: Myths about Intermittent Fasting 12
Chapter 4: Why Intermittent Fasting for Women over 50? 14
Chapter 5: Benefits of IF for Women over 50 17
Chapter 6: The One-Meal-a-Day Intermittent Fasting Diet 19
Chapter 7: Methods of Intermittent Fasting for Women over 50 23
Chapter 8: Starting with Intermittent Fasting 25
Chapter 9: Most Common Mistakes to Avoid 28
    Common Mistakes 28
        1. You're jumping into intermittent fasting too fast 28
        2. You're choosing the wrong plan for your lifestyle 28
        3. You're eating too much during the eating window 28
        4. You're not eating enough during the eating window 29
        5. Using it as an excuse to eat rubbish 29
        6. You're eating too many calories 29
        7. You're overanalyzing 30
        8. You're pushing yourself too hard 30
        9. Attempting to do too many things at once—over train, under eat and try fasting 30
        10. You're not drinking enough 30
        11. Giving up too soon 31
Chapter 10: Frequently Asked Questions about Intermittent Fasting 32
Chapter 11: The Right Mindset When Starting IF 36
Chapter 12: The Basics of Intermittent Fasting 38
    Must-Follow Guidelines 38
        1. Chart your progress 38
        2. Prep 38
        3. Breaking your fast 38
        5. Stay hydrated 38
        6. Weight loss 38
        7. Is breakfast vital? 39
        8. Drinks during no fast days 39
        9. Supplements 39
        10. Gender differences 39
        14. Constipation 40
        15. Affecting sleep 40
        16. Time-frame 40
        17. Do not rush 40
        1. Muscle cramps 40
        2. Heartburn 40
        3. Constipation 40
        4. Dizziness 40

Chapter 13: Basic of Eating on Intermittent Fasting 41
   Which Type of Food? 41
      1. Do Not Be Afraid To Think About Your Favorite Food 41
      2. Add Water 41
      3. Do Not Expect Weight Loss on Any Particular Day 41
      4. Be Wise, Be Careful, and Stop If You Feel Wrong 41
      5. Congratulations 41

Chapter 14: How to Practice: Step-by-Step Guide to Intermittent Fasting 44
   A Weekly Meal Plan Template 44
      Week 1 44
      Week 2 44
      Week 3 45
      Week 4 45

Chapter 15: Best Exercises for Women above 50 46

Chapter 16: Tips and Tricks for Staying Healthy 48

Chapter 17: Recipes 51
   Breakfast 51
      #1 Avocado Egg Bowls 51
      #2 Buttery Date Pancakes 52
      #3 Low Carb Pancake Crepes 53
      #4 Chia Seed Banana Blueberry Delight 54
      #5 Morning Meatloaf 55
      #6 Savory Breakfast Muffins 56
      #7 Low-Carb All Day Mexican Bowl 57
      #8 Speedy Low-Carb Tuna Lunch Bowl 58
      #9 Smoked Salmon, Avocado & Egg Lunch Bowl 59
      #10 Stir-Fried Pork with Ginger and Soy Sauce 60
      #11 Keto Crispy Ginger Mackerel Lunch Bawl 61
      #12 Italian Style Meatballs with Courgette 'Tagliatelle' 62
      #13 Creamy Tuscan Garlic Chicken 63
      #14 Turkey and Peppers 64
      #15 Shredded Chicken Chili 65
      #16 Taco Stuffed Avocados 66
      #17 Asparagus Stuffed Chicken 67
      #18 Ground Beef & Cabbage Stir Fry 68
      #19 Low-Carb Brownies 69
      #20 Apple Bread 70
      #21 Coconut Protein Balls 71
      #22 Protein Bars 72
      #23 Blueberry Muffins 73
      #24 Southwest Chicken Salad 74

Introduction

Intermittent fasting is a simple lifestyle change that can help in reversing several chronic illnesses. It is an age-old practice that humankind had been practicing for hundreds of thousands of years. Our bodies have evolved on this system, and hence they work the best with it.

Through the simple method of fasting and eating at certain intervals can help your systems in recovering from years of abuse that you have been subjecting them to. It is a comprehensive way to lose weight through the correct method, and that would also help in easing the burden from your body.

Intermittent fasting creates a system where your body can respond better to various changes. It also helps your organization in beginning the process of autophagy that can even start the self-healing process.

Two fundamental concepts that you will hear in this context are:

1.   Ketosis
2.   Autophagy

Ketosis: It is the process of burning fat for energy. Most people that are trying to lose weight fail to get any success or end up gaining more than they had ever suffered. This happens because they hadn't lost any weight in reality. Most of the time, the lost weight is just the water weight that their body loses to adjust to the current energy crisis. To lose real weight, your body would have to begin the process of ketosis. Intermittent fasting can help you at the beginning of this process quickly. Aided with a correct nutrition plan, you can expect ketosis to begin rapidly, and not only will your weight go down, but you will also experience fat-burning from your abdomen, thighs, and hips.

Autophagy: It is another term that you might have come across recently if you have been following the health news closely. It is a process of self-cleaning that your body is capable of carrying out under the right conditions. A study on this subject has helped a Japanese researcher win the 2016 Nobel Prize in medicine. This process can unlock the secret of longevity, health, and cure from some of the most untreatable conditions. The research on this subject has brought to light that under correct fasting conditions, the body can start purging all the inefficient processes, pathogens, and useless material inside the authority to make it more energy-efficient. This process can help in healing from several illnesses, and it also has potent anti-aging effects.

Both of these processes, combined with intermittent fasting, can help you in fighting most of the chronic illnesses in your body to a great extent.

Intermittent fasting is a positive lifestyle change that can help you in reversing the negative impact of chronic illnesses, and you can expect to live your future life in better health.

There are some of the most adamant health issues that we keep struggling with for most of our lives, but see no end to them. Intermittent fasting can also help you in fighting even those issues.

One such problem is obesity. Increasing weight and waistline is among the chief concerns of women of all age groups. However, it becomes a primary health concern of women in their 50s as it also starts affecting their overall health.

The first advice health care professionals give to overweight women is to control their weight to stay healthy. However, that's easy said than done.

Weight is adamant, and especially the belly fat simply refuses to go. Women, throughout their lives, try numerous methods but to no avail. Getting rid of weight is a big problem, but once you have lost some weight, preventing weight relapse is an even bigger problem.

Statistics show that more than 85% of women who had lost weight eventually regained more than they had lost.

Intermittent fasting can help you in getting freedom from this vicious cycle of gaining and losing weight. You can successfully lose weight and easily maintain it with the help of an intermittent fasting lifestyle.

Chapter 1: Intermittent Fasting Explained

Intermittent fasting is the technique of scheduling your dishes for your body to obtain the most out of them. Rather than minimizing your calorie use in fifty percent, refuting yourself of all the foods you value, or diving right into a classy diet plan pattern, intermittent fasting is an all-natural, logical, as well as healthy and also balanced method of eating that advertises fat burning. There are tons of ways to approach intermittent fasting.

It's defined as an eating pattern. This technique focuses on altering when you take in, instead of what you consume.

When you begin intermittent fasting, you will be more than likely to maintain your calorie intake the same; nonetheless, in contrast to spreading your dishes throughout the day, you will undoubtedly eat more significant recipes throughout a much shorter amount of time. As opposed to consuming 3 to 4 meals a day, you might eat one big meal at 11 A.M., afterward an added large dish at 6 P.M., without any dine-in between 11 A.M. and 6 P.M., as well as also after 6 P.M., no meal up until 11 the following day. This is simply one strategy of recurring fasting, and likewise, others will be-examined in this book in later stages.

Intermittent fasting is a technique used by whole lots of bodybuilders, specialist athletes, and also physical health and fitness masters to maintain their muscular tissue mass high and their body fat percent reduced. Recurring fasting can be done short term or long term, but the very best results originate from embracing this technique right into your everyday lifestyle.

The word "fasting" might stress the average person; intermittent fasting does not associate with starving yourself. To comprehend the principals behind effective intermittent fasting, we'll at first look through the body's digestion state: the fed state and the fasting state.

For 3 to 5 hours after consuming a meal, your body remains in what is described as the "fed state." Throughout the fed state, your insulin levels rise to soak up and digest your meal. When your insulin levels get high, it is exceptionally tough for your body to shed fat. Insulin is a hormone produced by the pancreatic to handle sugar degrees in the bloodstream. Its purpose is to manage insulin, it is technically a hormonal storage agent. When insulin degrees come to be so high, your body starts shedding your food for energy instead of your conserved fat. Which is why boosted degrees of it protect against weight reduction.

After the 3 to 5 hours are up, your body has finished refining the dish, and also you enter the post-absorptive state. The post-absorptive state lasts anywhere from 8 to 12 hours. When your body gets here, hereafter, the time room is the fasted state as a result of the reality that your body has refined your food by this.

Factor, your insulin levels are reduced, making your kept fat extremely available for losing.

Persisting fasting allows your body to get to an innovative weight loss state that you would usually obtain to with the average '3 meals daily' eating pattern. They are just altering the timing as well as the pattern of their food intake. It may take some time to get there when you start an intermittent fasting program right into the swing of points. Merely obtain back if you slip up right into your intermittent fasting pattern when you can.

Making a way of living adjustment entails a purposeful initiative, and also no one expects you to do it completely today. Intermittent fasting will definitely take some getting used to if you are not in the practice of going long periods without eating. As long as you pick the right technique for you, continue to be focused, and also remain concentrated, you will unanimously grasp it quickly.

Unlike some of the other diet regimen strategy that you may embark on, the intermittent fast is one that will certainly work. When you listen about it, it is simple to be a bit terrified regarding fasting.

Recurring fasting is a little bit various than you might assume. If you finish up being on, your body will often go right into hunger mode, rapid for as well lengthy.

You do not need to get as well concerned about exactly how this intermittent fast will work in the cravings mode. The intermittent fast is efficient because you are not going too quickly for as long that the body gets in right into this malnourishment setting as well as stops minimizing weight. Instead, it will make the fast continue long enough that you will have the ability to accelerate the metabolic process.

With the intermittent fast, you will discover that when you opt for a couple of hours without eating (usually no more than 2-4 hours), the body is not going to go right into the malnourishment setting. When complying with a recurring fasting plan, you require your body to melt more fat without placing in any sort-of extra job.

Here are a couple of fast pointers for success:

Mostly, it is essential not to expect to see outcomes from your new lifestyle promptly. Perhaps you need to focus on devoting to the process for a minimum of 30 days before you can start to evaluate the results correctly.

Second, it is imperative to remember that the excellent quality of the food you place into your body still matters as it will certainly merely take a few convenience food meals to reverse all of your tough work.

For the excellent results, you will plan to consist of an in-light exercise routine during fast days along with a far more fundamental regimen for full-calorie days. Intermittent fasting describes nutritional consuming patterns that include not consuming or continuous limiting calories for a long term period, intermittent fasting. There are various subgroups of regular fasting, each with variance in the duration of the fast of individuals, some for hours, others for a day. This has finished up being an extremely liked subject in the clinical research area as a result of every one of the prospective advantages of fitness in addition to health that is being found.

The diet regimen you adhere to whilst intermittent fasting will be figured out by the results that you are looking for and where you are beginning with additionally, so take a look at on your own and ask the question, "what do I want from this?"

If you are looking to lose a significant quantity of weight, then you are most likely to have to take a look at your diet regimen plan extra closely, yet if you wish to shed a couple of pounds for the beach, then you could discover that a pair of weeks of intermittent fasting can do that for you.

There are many various ways you can do intermittent fasting. We just are most likely to consider the 24-hour fasting system in which is what I used to shed 27 pounds over a 2-month duration. You could really feel some cravings pains, but these will also pass, as you end up being even more familiar with intermittent fasting, you might find as you have that feeling of need no more existing inside you without concern.

You might consider a juice made from celery, lime, broccoli, and also ginger, which will taste fantastic and also get some sufficient nutrient fluid into your body. It would be best to stick to the coffee, water, and tea if you can handle it.

Whatever your diet strategy is, whether it's healthy or not, you should see weight reduction after regarding three weeks of intermittent fasting, as well as do not be put off if you do not find much advancement at first, it's not a race, and also it is much far better to drop weight in a straight style over time, as opposed to losing a couple of extra pounds which you will put right back on. After the initial month, you might want to have an appearance at your diet plan on non-fasting days and also remove high sugar foods and even any scrap that you might generally take in. I have discovered that intermittent fasting over the long-term tends to make me wish to consume healthier foods as an all-natural routine.

If you are practicing intermittent fasting for bodybuilding, then you may wish to consider having a look at your macro-nutrients and also working out just how much healthy protein as well as carbohydrate you call for to eat, this is a lot more complex, as well as you can uncover info about this on several websites which you will need to spend time examining for the very best end results.

There are great deals of advantages to recurring fasting, which you will view as you proceed, a few of these advantages include even more energy, much less bloating, a clearer mind, and a basic feeling of wellness. It's important not to succumb to any type of lure to binge eat after a fasting duration, as this will negate the influence obtained from the recurring fasting period.

In verdict, simply by adhering to a two times a week 24-hour intermittent fasting approach for a couple of weeks, you will slim down, however, if you can boost your diet plan on the days that you do not want fast, then you will lose more weight, and if you can remain with this system, then you will certainly keep the weight off without turning to any kind of fad diet regimen or diet plans that are difficult to stick to.

Chapter 2: Benefits and Downsides of IF

There are just so many unexpected benefits of fasting, and while I'm sure you started reading this book hoping just to lose weight with fasting, you can gain so many more health benefits than just weight loss. Unfortunately, there's nothing perfect in life, and I'm sad to say that intermittent fasting isn't perfect. There are always some risks and drawbacks of fasting.

While reading these benefits and risks, keep in mind that not everyone will react the same way. How you react to fasting isn't going to be the same as how someone else does. So, look at your health with a critical eye and consider whether the benefits will help you or whether the risks will harm you. You can also just do a trial and error fast to see how your body will react, but always do so with wisdom.

It's important to mention some of the limitations of these studies. Intermittent fasting is so recent that there isn't enough research yet on the human experience while intermittent fasting. There is some research, but not a lot. More research has been done on animals that are like humans biologically, like some apes. Some less similar animals are rodents, and there are a lot of studies on fasting with rodents. Some of these will be mentioned here, and some will be human studies. But all will help explain the benefits and risks.

Benefits of Intermittent Fasting

Generally, intermittent fasting has way more benefits than risks. The one everyone knows about is weight loss. But there are so many other benefits too. One of the best benefits is how intermittent fasting changes your hormone levels so that your insulin levels are lowered. There are also some other benefits for your heart, brain, and body.

Weight Loss

It is the most well-known benefit of intermittent fasting. During intermittent fasting, it's likely that you'll lose some weight. Whether you're following the easier 14/10 method or the harder alternate day method, you're going to lose some weight. There are a couple of reasons why this is, but the biggest one is because of calorie restriction.

Calorie restriction is one of the most common methods of weight loss recommended by doctors. In simplified 14/10 fasts and ones like it, you'll have some unplanned calorie restriction that can help you with weight loss. To get the most out of calorie restriction, you would want to follow the alternate day style of fasting. This is because there's just such a massive reduction in calories on those alternate days. Alternate day fasting has been found to be equivalent to regular, doctor-approved, calorie reduction in multiple studies (Alhamdan et al., 2016; Klemple et al., 2010; Anson et al., 2003). Even better yet, because calorie reduction is interspersed with full regular meals every other day, this style of fasting is easier to stick with rather than a regular calorie-restricted diet.

So, you can expect some weight loss while intermittent fasting. However, this also depends on other aspects of your lifestyle. We've talked about the importance of diet before, but we haven't talked about the importance of exercising. Doing regular exercising while intermittent fasting can also increase how much weight you lose, without losing a lot of muscle mass from the fast. You don't have to exercise heavily, but if you want to, you could go for a 30-minute walk, a bike ride, or a swim. All of these can help maintain your weight loss while also maintaining your muscle mass. The last thing to mention is that once you finish your fasting, in the case where you're not doing this for the rest of your life, you'll be less likely to regain the weight. Take it or leave it, but you'll still have some improvement in your weight with intermittent fasting.

Intermittent fasting can reduce insulin levels and insulin resistance. Did you know that one-third of Americans are diagnosed with pre-diabetes? That's quite a lot and is often due to our carb and sugar-laden diets—so many people in the U.S. struggle with their blood sugar levels and insulin levels. Essentially, in prediabetes, your blood sugar levels are consistently higher than normal, and your body tries to fix this by increasing your insulin. Insulin is what helps your body to absorb the glucose from your food to use as energy. However, when experiencing prediabetes, your cells become resistant to insulin. This increases the cycle again, with more insulin coming into your bloodstream and more insulin resistance occurring. This can be very problematic and result in having a diagnosis of type 2 diabetes, stroke, obesity, or heart disease. Intermittent fasting can help with your insulin levels and insulin resistance.

When intermittent fasting, the blood glucose levels can be a little more controlled, insulin resistance is reduced, and insulin itself is also reduced. This is something that has been repeated in several studies. The insulin decreases because of the way the body uses glucose from eating during the fasting period, but it also decreases because of weight loss that is also happening. In most studies, the type of fasting used to create some of the best changes in insulin levels was alternate day fasting. This makes a lot of sense since it's also the style of fasting that results in the most weight loss.

Improved heart health is one of the benefits that need to be better researched in humans. However, in animals, intermittent fasting is very promising for improving heart health. Intermittent fasting helps improve cholesterol levels, blood pressure, and inflammation. All of which can lead to better heart health. Obviously, this is important since there are so many things that can negatively affect heart health. So, if intermittent fasting can help reduce these things, then you'll have a lower risk of heart disease, heart attacks, and other cardiovascular problems.

Some research suggests intermittent fasting can help with aging and brain health. It has to do with how your cells recuperate from cellular stress and metabolism. The study suggests that intermittent fasting can help reduce the likelihood of Alzheimer's and Parkinson's diseases (Martin et al., 2009). While this research is up-and-coming, there hasn't been enough human research to say this. However, the promise of better brain health is something to look forward to with intermittent fasting.

Risks of Intermittent Fasting

The risks of intermittent fasting are varied. If people fast when they shouldn't, then the dangers of intermittent fasting can be quite severe. However, for most people, intermittent fasting isn't very risky. The risks you'll run into are bingeing, malnutrition, and difficulty with maintaining the fast. We've talked about bingeing quite extensively, so we're not going to discuss it much more. Suffice it to say, bingeing while you fast risks any of the benefits from fasting you might initially have. A more significant risk is malnutrition.

Malnutrition sounds alarming, but for the most part, you can prevent this by having well-balanced meals during your eating windows. The risk of malnutrition comes especially during the kinds of fast, which includes the very-low-calorie restriction on fasting days. Fasts like this are 5:2 fasts and alternate-day fasting. If you're not eating the right nutrition throughout your week, the reduction in calories plus the poor diet can result in some of your dietary needs not being met. This could result in more weight loss but also more muscle loss and other issues. To prevent this risk, you can ensure that your meals are nutritious and well-balanced. Have a variety of fruits and vegetables, try different meats and seafood, and include grains unless you're following a specific diet like the keto diet.

Associated with malnutrition is dehydration. We get a lot of our daily water intake from the food we eat. But if you're eating a reduced amount of food during your day, or no food during your day, you're going to need to drink a lot more water than you usually do. If you're not keeping track of your hydration levels, it's possible for you to drink too little. To combat this risk, ensure that you're drinking enough by keeping a hydration journal. You could also track it in an app. Set up reminders to drink water and check your urine color. Light-colored urine means proper hydration, so check often despite how disgusting it might be for you.

Because fasting can be challenging to start, this can be one of the risks associated with it. You're going to feel hungry during the first couple of weeks of following your fasting schedule. You may even feel uncomfortable, with mood swings, different bowel movements, and sleep disruptions. All of this can lead to you struggling with starting the fasts. They can also lead you to ignore more significant warning signs that you shouldn't fast. These signs include changed heart rate, feelings of weakness, and extreme fatigue. These feelings shouldn't be ignored during the start. If you feel severely uncomfortable when you start your fast, you should stop and speak with your doctor.

Chapter 3: Myths about Intermittent Fasting

There are so many myths about intermittent fasting circulating in health books and on the internet. These erroneous statements have created a stigma around intermittent fasting that causes people to avoid following this breakthrough diet. Learn to see through these myths which are not valid.

Fasting Is Dangerous

This first myth is merely ridiculous. Everyone intermittently fasts as they sleep. Doing it at other times or for a few days on end is no more dangerous than merely fasting while you sleep. The body needs a period to perform autophagy, and it cannot do that if it is too busy processing food all of the time. Intermittent fasting gives your body a well-deserved break while helping you preserve your health. Remember, fasting is not starvation. You can still eat. Don't confuse fasting, which is healthful, with starvation, which is dangerous.

Fasting Can Lower Your Blood Sugar Dangerously

The body can maintain its blood glucose levels by releasing glycogen or sugar stored in the liver. This fact means that you won't go low dangerously if you stop eating for a spell. Instead, it will balance out and cause your body to start burning fat. The fat will keep you nourished and prevent fainting from not eating.

If you feel faint or lightheaded, you may need to eat. Be sure to listen to your body. Decrease your fasting period if you keep having dizzy spells.

However, if you are diabetic or hypoglycemic, you may need some help to maintain blood sugars during fasting. Ask your doctor how you can do this maintenance. Some fruit juice will technically break your fast, but it is necessary if your blood glucose plummets down.

It Will Cause Hormonal Imbalance

If anything, IF will balance your hormones. Doing IF wrong will indeed cause leptin and ghrelin, the main hunger hormones, to go crazy and make people binge. Then they will feel guilty and restrict themselves more. The hormones will get even more imbalanced. This effect can suppress a woman's ovulation and even stop her period. However, a woman who implements IF correctly by keeping herself nourished in her eating windows will not experience this at all.

It Will Destroy Your Metabolism

Your metabolism will run on whatever energy source is easiest. Sugar from food is the easiest, so your body burns that first. With no sugar present, the body turns to burn its own fat cells. Either way, your metabolism works. You cannot destroy it. Some say that if you fast, you will overeat and then have even more trouble losing weight. This problem is psychological, not physiological. Often people hate restrictive diets so much that they do overeat when they stop dieting, causing them to gain the weight back. Then, they are resistant to new diet approaches and have trouble losing the regained weight. Affecting over 80% of people who have dieted, this problem is pretty common. But if you stick with IF and nourish yourself properly, you won't return to overeating, and you won't have this problem, IF doesn't ruin your metabolism to the point where you can't lose weight again, if you do gain any back.

It Causes Stress
Technically, fasting is a period of stress. But as Dr. Fung points out, it is good stress that causes your cells to do their work more efficiently and handle the stress of illness more successfully. Therefore, fasting will not cause extra stress.
The first week or so can be stressful because the approach involves change. Relax a lot and do things you enjoy or find soothing. The stress will pass.

Fasting Can Lead to Overeating
If executed with care, you can avoid the urge to binge eat later. Fasting will indeed make you hungry because of your body's hunger signals. You may feel the urge to eat more when you can or cheat on your fast. The key here is to keep yourself well-nourished when you do eat. Use bone broth to stave off cravings during fasting periods. Also, avoid going on long fasts when you first start. Don't allow the temptation of food around you or have lots of easy snacks in the house as you fast.

Fasting Causes the Body to Go into Starvation Mode
Starvation mode is a myth that some people believe causes the body to hold onto weight when it perceives that it is not getting sufficient calories. Look at any person who has starved themselves, and you will see rapid, immediate weight loss and wasting. That picture of starvation proves that restricting calories to dangerous levels will not cause weight gain, but rather weight loss. Plus, fasting is not a dangerous caloric restriction or starvation, so it will not cause any unhealthy "mode."

Fasting Causes the Body to Burn Muscle
Because fasting stimulates the production of HGH, it builds muscle rather than destroys it. It only promotes your body to eat fat, not muscle. People tend to start losing muscle mass if they consume too few calories, or essentially starve themselves. But they will not lose muscle if they stay nourished and hydrated and eat well between fasting periods.

You Can't Work Out While Fasting
You can work out while fasting. If you have eaten well during your eating window and have some extra body fat, exercise will only make your body burn more. Your body will get the nutrition it needs to fuel the workout from your fat stores and the last meal you ate. Be sure to stay hydrated for energy.

Chapter 4: Why Intermittent Fasting for Women over 50?

There are plenty of diets out there, all promising you the impossible—incredible weight loss, with no mention of any side effects. You are probably fed up with the "lose x pounds in 30 days, guaranteed" approach. Many of these diets are not backed up by science, or in other words, there is not any scientific research to prove these diets deliver what they promise. They focus only on the weight loss process, suggesting meal plans that are incredibly radical in some cases.

Diets mean nutrient deprivation in most cases, but they are plenty of instances where these diets have harmful effects on your health. Unlike other diets, focusing on the weight loss process in an incredibly short amount of time, intermittent fasting is focusing more on your health, as nutritionists believe that health should be the most important factor, and only a healthy body can have a long and sustainable weight loss process unlike the other diets, which have a "hit and run" approach, IF is something for the long run and should be regarded as a way of life, not like a meal plan to be implemented for a few weeks. By checking out the benefits below, you can better understand why this process is so beneficial for your body.

The main benefits of intermittent fasting can be summarized in 8 points:
- Eliminates precancerous and cancerous cells
- Shifts quickly into nutritional ketosis
- Reduces the fat tissue
- Enhances the gene expression for healthspan and longevity
- Induces autophagy and the apoptotic cellular repair or cleaning
- Improves your insulin sensitivity
- Reduces inflammation and oxidative stress
- Increases neuroprotection and cognitive effects

To expand on the benefits of this practice, intermittent fasting can have positive impacts over the fat loss process, disease prevention, anti-aging, therapeutic benefits (psychological, spiritual, and physical), mental performance, physical fitness (improved metabolism, wind, and endurance, the significant effect over bodybuilding).

Intermittent Fasting for the Weight Loss Process

As you restrain yourself from eating, the body will no longer have available glucose to use to produce energy. Therefore, it will use ketones to break the fat tissue open and release the energy stored in there. This is how the body will burn your existing fat in order to generate energy. When it comes to diets, they are not designed for the long run, and as soon as you break the diet, you will start gaining weight again. Intermittent fasting is something that you can try for a lifetime because it is easy to stick to it, and it doesn't involve any special meal plan. So, you can still eat your favorite foods, as long as you schedule your meals, allowing a smaller eating window and a longer fasting period, IF induces ketosis and eventually autophagy, which will definitely mean reducing the fat reserves.

Intermittent Fasting for Preventing Diseases

What if you found out that intermittent fasting is, in fact, a cure for several different diseases and medical conditions? You would definitely become more interested in this process. There are a few studies that show the beneficial effects IF has on your health. A study published in the World Journal of Diabetes has shown that patients with type 2 diabetes on short-term daily intermittent fasting experience a lower body weight, but also a better variability of post-meal glucose.

Other benefits this diet has are:
- Enhances the markers of stress resistance
- Reduces blood pressure and inflammation
- Better lipid levels and glucose circulation, which may lead to a lower risk of cardiovascular disease, neurological diseases like Parkinson's and Alzheimer's, and also cancer

Intermittent Fasting for the Anti-aging Process

The modern-day lifestyle includes too much stress and is too sedentary. Whether we like it or not, these factors have a great contribution to the aging process. You are probably wondering what intermittent fasting can do the slow down this process, as we all know that it can't be stopped. IF is not "the fountain of youth," and it will not grant you immortality, but it can still lower the blood pressure and reduce oxidative damage, enhance your insulin sensitivity and reduce your fat mass. Coincidence or not, all of these are factors that are known to improve your health and longevity. Intermittent fasting is one of the triggering factors of autophagy, a process known for destroying and replacing old cell parts with new ones, at any level within your body. Such a process can slow down the aging process.

Intermittent Fasting Practiced for Therapeutic Benefits

When it comes to therapeutic benefits, the most important ones are physical, spiritual, and psychological. In terms of physical benefits, intermittent fasting is a powerful cure for diabetes, but it can also prove to be very useful for reducing seizure-related brain damage and seizures themselves, but also for improving the symptoms of arthritis. This practice also has a spiritual value, as it's widely practiced for religious purposes across the globe. Although fasting is regarded as penance by some practitioners, it's also a practice for purifying your body and soul (according to the religious approach).

Intermittent fasting is also about exercising control and will over your body and your feelings. Achieving absolute control over your power and mind is a very powerful psychological benefit. You can ignore hunger; restrain yourself from eating for a certain period of time. In other words, IF is also associated with mind training and can also improve your self-esteem. A successful intermittent fasting regime can have very powerful effects from a psychological point of view. A study has shown that women practicing IF had amazing results in terms of senses of control, reward, pride, and achievement.

Intermittent Fasting for Better Mental Performance

IF also enhances the cognitive function and also is very useful when it comes to boosting your brainpower. There are several factors of intermittent fasting, which can support this claim. First of all, it boosts the level of brain-derived neurotrophic factor (also known as BDNF), which is a protein in your brain that can interact with the parts of your brain responsible for controlling cognitive and memory functions, as well as learning. BDNF can even protect and stimulate the growth of new brain cells. Through IF, you will enter the ketogenic state, during which your body turns fat into energy, by using ketones. Ketones can also feed your brain, and therefore improve your mental acuity, productivity, and energy.

Intermittent Fasting for an Improved Physical Fitness
This process influences not only your brain but also your digestive system. By setting a small feeding window and a larger fasting period, you will encourage the proper digestion of food. This leads to a proportional and healthy daily intake of food and calories. The more you get used to this process, the less you will experience hunger. If you are worried about slowing your metabolism, think again! IF enhances your metabolism, it makes metabolism more flexible, as the body has now the capability to run on glucose or fats for energy, in a very effective way. In other words, intermittent fasting leads to better metabolism.

Oxygen use during exercise is a crucial part of the success of your training. You simply can't have performance without adjusting your breathing habits during workouts. VO_2 max represents the maximum amount of oxygen your body can use per minute or per kilogram of body weight. In popular terms, VO_2 max is also referred to as "wind." The more oxygen you use, the better you will be able to perform. Top athletes can have twice the VO_2 level of those without any training. A study focused on the VO_2 levels of a fasted group (they just skipped breakfast) and a non-fasted group (they had breakfast an hour before). For both groups, the VO_2 level was at 3.5 L/min at the beginning, and after the study, the level showed a significant increase of "wind" for the fasting group (9.7%), compared to just 2.5% increase in the case of those with breakfast.

Intermittent Fasting for Bodybuilding
Having a narrow feeding window automatically means fewer meals so that you can concentrate the daily calorie intake into just 1-2 consistent meals. Bodybuilders find this approach a lot more pleasing than having the same calorie consumption split into 5 or 6 different meals throughout the day. It's said that you need a specific amount of proteins just to maintain your muscle mass. However, muscle mass can also be maintained through intermittent fasting, a process that doesn't focus specifically on protein intake. Remember, the growth hormone reaches unbelievable levels after 48 hours of fasting, so you can easily maintain your muscles without eating many proteins, or having protein bars or shakes.

As you already know, nothing is perfect and intermittent fasting is no exception. There are a few side effects that you need to worry about, like:

- Hunger is perhaps the most common side effect of this way of eating, but the more you get used to IF, the less hunger you will feel
- Beware of constipation, as when you eat less, you will not have to go to the toilet very often, so you can feel constipated at the beginning
- Headaches should be expected when fasting. Food deprivation is a direct cause of these headaches. However, controlling your hunger and getting used to fasting will be the best weapon to fight against these headaches
- During intermittent fasting, you might experience muscle cramps, heartburn, and dizziness
- In the case of athletic women or those with very low body fat percentage, intermittent fasting may lead to a higher risk of irregular periods and lower chances of conception (so it reduces fertility for these women)

Chapter 5: Benefits of IF for Women over 50

Studies have shown that intermittent fasting may be extremely useful for postmenopausal women to aid in maintaining their weight. There are quite a few benefits to intermittent fasting for middle-aged women or women that are going through menopause no matter their age.

Why for Women over 50?

Women who approach post-menopause (and sometimes even as early as pre-menopause) tend to start accumulating belly fat. They will start noticing their metabolism gets slower. They may also start feeling aches and pains in their joints. Their sleep patterns start to get completely out of routine, leaving them feeling exhausted all the time. Then there is the weight gain and also a higher risk of developing chronic diseases like cancer, diabetes, and heart disease that could lead to heart attacks.

There is also the risk of neurodegenerative diseases, stroke, and a constant feeling of fatigue. Intermittent fasting has been known to reset a person's internal balance. This, in turn, boosts their external appearance, energy levels, and cuts down on stress as they control their weight.

Why Should Women Choose the Intermittent Fasting Diet?

Intermittent fasting has become a very popular healthy lifestyle trend, and for a good reason. It offers many health benefits as well as improves a person's state of mind and encourages an all-round feeling of well-being.

Benefits of Intermittent Fasting for Women over 50

When women get to 50 and over, their skin will start to show signs of age. They may find their joints begin to ache for no reason, and suddenly belly fat accumulates as if you have just given birth. There are so many creams, diets, and exercises on the market to tighten the skin and try to help. The fact is, they may work to a certain point, but then the body hits a shelf, and nothing seems to push a person past it. This boils up frustration, making women look into the more radical and costly alternatives like surgery. Which in itself poses so many more dangers and risks for women of 50 and over.

A person does not need to go under the knife or starve themselves to reboot their system or change their shape. Intermittent fasting is a much cheaper and less risky way to do this, and there is no need to make any drastic eating habit changes either. Well, you may need to make a few adjustments, like cutting out junk food and eating healthier. But once again, the diet a person follows is their personal choice and depends on how serious they are about becoming healthier.

Some health benefits of intermittent fasting for women over 50 include:

Activating Cellular Repair

Fasting has been known to kick start the body's natural cellular repair function, get rid of mature cells, improve longevity, and improve hormone function. All things that tend to take a battering as people age. This can alleviate joint and muscle aches as well as lower back pain. As the cells are being repaired and the damage is undone, it helps with the skin's elasticity and health too.

Increase Cognitive Function and Protects the Brain from Damage
Intermittent fasting may increase the levels of a brain hormone known as a brain-derived neurotrophic factor (BDNF). It may equally guard the brain against damage like a stroke or Alzheimer's disease as it promotes new nerve cell growth. It also increases cognitive function and could effectively defend a person against other neurodegenerative diseases as well.

Weight Loss
When people have belly fat, it can cause many health problems that are associated with various diseases, as it indicates a person has visceral fat. Visceral fat is fat that goes deep into the abdominal surrounding the organs. Belly fat is hard to lose, especially for an aging woman. Intermittent fasting has been known to help reduce not only weight but inches of over five percent of body fat in around twenty-two to twenty-five weeks (Barna, 2019).

Alleviates Oxidative Stress and Inflammation
Oxidative stress is when the body has an imbalance of antioxidants as well as free radicals. This imbalance can cause both tissue and cell damage in overweight as well as aging people. It can also lead to various chronic illnesses like cancer, heart disease, diabetes, and has an impact on the signs of aging. Oxidative stress can trigger the inflammation that causes these diseases.

Intermittent fasting can provide your system with a reboot, helping to alleviate oxidative stress and inflammation in a middle-aged woman. It also significantly reduces the risk of oxidative stress and inflammation for those overweight or obese.

Slow down the Aging Process
As intermittent fasting gives both the metabolism and cellular repair a reboot, it offers the potential to slow down aging. It may even prolong a person's lifespan by quite a few years, especially if following a nutritious diet and exercise regime alongside intermittent fasting.

Chapter 6: The One-Meal-a-Day Intermittent Fasting Diet

Naturally, carrying out this reduction process leads you to eat one meal per day with no consumption "window" at all. A limiting process that continually shrinks the consumption window can be applied, while still maintaining the goal of getting food every day. In other words, why not simply eat just once every twenty-four hours? The principles of the one-meal-a-day approach are very straightforward. You simply follow these rules:

- **Fasting period:** You fast for 23 hours each day. During this time, you only consume liquids that have zero or very little calories. Most people will limit themselves to water and perhaps tea or coffee. It's important to note if you choose to drink tea or coffee because they are diuretics, and keeping up your water consumption during fasting is important. In addition, some people will drink bone broth while fasting, which may provide a small number of calories. However, the calories in bone broth can be considered negligible, and people are drinking bone broth to get the mineral content and not for calories.
- **Eating period:** You consume your one meal a day in a time window of 60 minutes or less.

Eating one meal a day has more benefits than first meets the eye. Certainly, doing so will give you a larger amount of time in the actual fasted state than what you will get having a large consumption window of up to eight hours. However, there is a second benefit in that you are going to be consuming less food. You can have a large meal during your 60-minute window, but there is only so much you can eat in one sitting even if you gorge yourself. As a result, your total caloric intake will be reduced even if you're eating a large amount during your meal as compared to following a 16:8 type of intermittent fasting.

Scientific research has shown that reduced-calorie diets can increase longevity while slowing down the aging process. However, a reduced-calorie diet comes with some downsides. People who follow a reduced-calorie diet find that they have less energy, feel cold, and have a lower libido. Typically, a person following a reduced-calorie diet will limit their total calorie intake to something like 800 calories per day. A one-meal-a-day intermittent fasting program will naturally limit calories consumed, but the reality is that there is no official limit of calorie intake. You can eat until you are satisfied during your 60-minute time window. A reduced-calorie diet will slow the metabolism, but that isn't the goal of intermittent fasting.

Calorie reduction not only slows the aging process; it has shown that limiting calorie intake by around 15% for an extended period lowers the risk of contracting many chronic "Western" diseases, including cancer, heart disease, Alzheimer's disease, and dementia. It is believed that these benefits stem from a slower metabolism, which results from being in a chronic state of consuming reduced calories. When the metabolism slows, there is less production of damaging free radicals.

Calorie reduction carried out over an extended period obviously leads to weight loss. As a result, many of the benefits attributed to radical calorie-restrictive diets may be due to the simple fact that people who follow it are avoiding the problems that follow from being overweight and obese.

However, there are far better ways to get fit and maintain a healthy weight, such as following a keto or paleo diet.

Something people who promote calorie-restricted diets miss is that when you consume food, you are going to be replenishing glycogen in your liver, and blood sugars are going to rise. Typically, calorie-restricted diets are advised without any regard for food content. If you are consuming carbohydrates on a calorie-restricted diet, then you are going to be utilizing blood sugar for energy. Weight loss will happen due to calorie deprivation, but you will not get the benefits that you will from outright fasting or from following a keto or low-carb diet, such as Atkins.

There are four ways that medical professionals measure calorie burning. The first way is called the basal metabolic rate or BMR. This is the rate at which calories are burned in order to maintain vital bodily functions. It is the minimal number of calories that your body needs to burn to keep the brain functioning, maintain heart rate, and keep you breathing. Put another way, BMR is the minimum necessary to get oxygen, pump blood, and stay conscious.

Other ways that calories are burned are called thermic effects. Simply moving around causes the burning of calories, whether you are getting up to move from one chair to another or engaging in exercise. That type of calorie burning is called the thermic effect of exercise—that is, calories burned while engaging in physical activity.

Related to this is "NEAT," which is a measure of calories burned in incidental movements, such as twiddling your thumbs. Nobody ever sits completely still, and if you watch a room full of high school students sitting at desks, you will notice that they are constantly fidgeting. This is called non-exercise activity thermogenesis (NEAT)—calories burned from fidgeting or moving around without getting up and utilizing your large muscle groups. For the most part, this type of activity occurs on a subconscious level, and younger people will burn more calories this way than older people who have "slowed down."

Another basic way you burn calories is by eating. Digestion is an active process, so it is going to burn off some calories. In fact, you burn up to 10% of the calories you consume by simply digesting a meal. This is called the thermal effect of food.

In summary, a calorie-restricted diet is more akin to entering a starvation state than it is too intermittent fasting. The so-called starvation mode is a state the body enters when it feels it needs to conserve energy in response to a food-deprived state that can lead to the loss of life. If there is less energy coming into the body, then it attempts to maintain a balance by reducing energy expenditure, i.e., by slowing down the metabolism. The body will attempt to fight back, and in the short term will increase the sensation of hunger in order to motivate you to seek out and consume some calories.

Calorie restriction causes the levels of four hormones in your body to decrease. The first of these is the thyroid hormone. This hormone is important for maintaining the basal metabolic rate. Higher levels of the thyroid hormone will result in more oxygen consumption and energy utilization and lead to the production of more body heat. Deficiencies in the thyroid hormone are not normal and are treated by medical professionals for reasons outside the scope of this book; however, one thing to note is that people with lower levels of the thyroid hormone can have slightly lower body temperatures. Following a reduced-calorie diet can cause levels of the thyroid hormone to drop.

A reduced-calorie diet can also cause levels of a hormone called leptin to drop. Leptin is made by fat cells and acts inside your brain in a region called the hypothalamus. Leptin tends to inhibit hunger, so a drop in leptin levels can increase the sensation of hunger. You can see from this that a drop in leptin levels is part of the body's response of trying to get you to eat when it is faced with a reduced intake of calories.

Finally, when following a reduced-calorie diet, you will see a reduction in levels of the hormone norepinephrine. You can think of this hormone as a "fight or flight" hormone—in other words, it gets the body ready for taking action.

Seeing how the hormones impacted by a reduced-calorie diet act on the body, you can understand that someone following a constant reduced-calorie diet will be basically operating in a slowed down and semi-lethargic state. All dieting, of course, involves some level of calorie reduction. However, the levels of calorie consumption in the course of everyday life in modern societies involve the consumption of far more calories than we need. Second, a diet like a keto naturally restricts calories without entering a starvation state. When you follow a diet like a keto, you eat what your body needs, but you are not entering a state of starvation like that advocated by practitioners of a calorie-restricted diet, and so you won't end up in a slowed down semi-deprived state.

One side effect of a strictly reduced-calorie diet—and that many people are put off by—is that it inevitably means a reduction of muscle mass. When the body faces continual deprivation in calories that are so low that they are near the level of actual starvation, the body will begin burning its own protein, which means it is going to burn your muscle mass. This causes further weight loss and slows the metabolism even more—since muscle tissue burns more energy over a given time frame than other tissues. If you think of the person following one of these extreme reduced-calorie diets as a sickly looking thin college professor with gray hair, a beard, and glasses, you are not far off the mark. However, when you are following a one-meal-a-day diet, you can avoid the problem of consuming your muscle mass by eating plenty of protein during your meal. Remember that protein intake is vital for the body to continue functioning, and it has to get protein from somewhere. In the absence of adequate protein intake, the body will break down muscle mass because the normal bodily processes that require proteins must continue in order to stay alive.

Those people who are utilizing the power of intermittent fasting are looking to achieve the health benefits of fasting without entering a starvation state, so looking to reduce calorie burning and slow the metabolism massively is not on the list of things to achieve. In fact, many people who are using intermittent fasting as a tool are looking to have a higher metabolism rather than entering a slowed down, restricted metabolism state of near starvation. Voluntarily restricting calories to a near-starvation level to increase lifespan actually sounds like a bad tradeoff.

Why would you want an extended lifespan if you are a thin, slowed-down shell of a person? It turns out that by using intermittent fasting, we can get many of the benefits of a reduced-calorie diet but without the downsides.

With weight loss comes some reduction of calorie expenditure. When you have less body tissue, you are simply burning fewer calories. Someone who weighs 200 pounds will burn more calories than someone who weighs 150 pounds by merely going through the days' activities and existing. Of course, you will get a headache if you try and figure out how many calories you're burning, and that is a detail you don't need to concern yourself with anyway. The only rule to be aware of is that it takes a deficit of 3,500 calories to burn off a pound of fat—or put another way, a pound of body fat stores 3,500 calories.

Chapter 7: Methods of Intermittent Fasting for Women over 50

There are various ways you could engage in intermittent fasting. These types have been proven to give the same effects that have made people start fasting, and some of these potentials benefits include the loss of weight and fat. Some have also discovered that it helps in reducing the risk of getting some diseases.

These are some of the types that are popular and have been proven to show effectiveness:

The 16/8 Method

This method requires a daily fast of 14 hours for women and 16 hours for men. You'll have to limit the times you eat to a total of 8 to 10-hour eating window. With this method, you can incorporate 2 to 3 or more meals in a day.

Martin Berkhan, the famous fitness expert, made this method popular. Some refer to it as the Lean-Gains protocol. It is the most popular because it is almost natural. The hours you skip meals fall under the time you are either sleeping or working. Most people who skip their breakfast and finish dinner before eight are actually doing the 16-hour protocol, but they don't know that.

Women are advised to fast for 14 to 15 hours because most do better with this short-range, and during the fast, you have to eat healthy foods during the eating window. The results you want to achieve won't be forthcoming if there's a lot of junk in your food.

You can take water and coffee during the fasting hours as well as other drinks that are no caloric. To fast with this method, your last meal should be by 8 P.M. while your first meal should be by noon.

The 5:2 Diet

British journalist Michael Mosley popularized this method. It has also been called the fast diet.

This method requires that you limit the number of calories you consume to only 500 for females and 600 for male two days a week. That means you usually eat for five days and reduce the calories in your diet for two days.

For example, you might eat every day of the week except Tuesday and Thursday, where you reduce the food you consume. You limit the calories for breakfast to 250 for women and 300 for men while dinner takes the same number of calories as well.

Eat-Stop-Eat

This method requires you to do a 24-hour fast either once or twice a week, whichever one is comfortable for you.

An example is not eating from 7 p.m. to 7 p.m. the next day. That is if you start with dinner on Monday, you don't eat from 7 p.m. Monday until 7 p.m. Tuesday. You can do this once or twice a week. If it is once, it should be done mid-week, like Wednesday, and if it is twice, it is good if the days are spread apart, e.g., Monday and Thursday.

You can drink water, coffee, and other no caloric drinks between fasting periods, but solid foods are not allowed. It is, however, not advisable to start with this method as it requires a lot of energy for long hours without food. Start with 16 hours fasting before plunging into the 24 hours fast.

Alternate-Day Fasting
Most of the health benefits that were revealed are as a result of this method. That is fasting on alternate days.
There are two variations to this method:
a)   24-hour full day fasting every other day. This requires you to normally eat for a day and then fast for the next 24 hours.
b)   Eating only a few hundred calories. The alternate-day fasting can be very challenging, and this made the experts devise another plan where you only eat a reduced number of calories every other day.
An example is that when you fast on Monday, you normally eat on Tuesday, fast on Wednesday, and continue for the rest of the week.

The Warrior Diet
This method of fasting was made famous by Ori Hofmekler, another fitness expert. This diet requires you to fast or eat a small or little chunk of food during the day while consuming a huge meal at night, a typical case of fast and feast later. You eat small amounts of fruits and vegetables during the day and fall back to a huge meal. The meal is best eaten by 4 p.m. in the evening. No food must be eaten until the next morning when you continue with fruits and vegetables.
A feast for dinner and fast for the day.

Spontaneous Meal Skipping
This is a more natural method than the 16/8 because there's no routine. You just skip meals when convenient.
This can be done in some instances, such as when you are not really hungry or are on a journey and can't find suitable food to eat. You can skip these meals.
There's no routine to this method. You can decide to skip your meal anytime, from lunch to dinner to breakfast. Once you don't follow a routine, you are using this method.
These methods, however, are not suitable for every individual, and you don't need to try everything before you know which is ideal for you.
This guide is for women over 50 years old, and this kind of people often lose energy more rapidly than typical younger youths, so methods such as the alternate-day fasting and the eat-stop-eat method are not suitable for women over fifty because these types and processes require a lot of energy, which these women lack.
The 16/8 is not suitable for every one woman over fifty, but it's a good start if you want to take the fast to another level. There's no magic to it, and no one can tell you what's best for you. You have to discover yourself.
The spontaneous meal skipping is a great place to start, but the results won't be as fast as the other methods because of the lack of routine.
The best methods, however, are the eat-stop-eat and the 5:2. These two have routines you can follow, but you don't need to stay away from food, only consume small calories. This way, you fast with a routine, and the results will be achieved.
Whichever you decide to use, make sure you consult your doctor to see if intermittent fasting is suitable for you.

Chapter 8: Starting with Intermittent Fasting

Before trying out intermittent fasting, you have to find out whether it will work for you first. You have to determine if this eating pattern is appropriate for you first based on your present weight, lifestyle, body type, and health condition.

Note that even if it has plenty of benefits when done properly, like regulating your blood glucose, managing your body weight, gaining or maintaining lean muscle mass, and controlling blood lipids, it is not suitable for everyone. If you are still unsure, you may want to consult your doctor first.

Seek his advice and find out if your health will not get drastically affected by your decision to try intermittent fasting. In most cases, though, intermittent fasting seems to produce favorable and successful results for those who have the following or belong to any of the following:

- Have a history of monitoring food and calorie intake
- Have enough experience in terms of working out
- Single or without children
- Have a supportive partner—someone who supports your decision to try IF
- Have a job that lets you have low-performance periods while adapting to a new eating pattern or plan
- Obtained a go-signal from your doctor to try IF

Intermittent fasting can also greatly benefit those who intend to lose weight. In fact, weight loss is one factor that encouraged most practitioners of this eating pattern to give it a try.

However, take note that while there are those who can greatly benefit from intermittent fasting, some should also avoid it as much as possible. It does not seem to work well for those who are underweight or dealt with eating disorders in the past. You can still try it, though, but you have to get the go-signal of a health professional first.

It is not also highly recommended for those who are:

- Pregnant
- Suffering from chronic stress
- Having sleeping disorders
- Still new in terms of dieting and exercising

If you are still a beginner when it comes to dieting and working out, you may think that intermittent fasting is the best solution for you if your goal is to lose weight. However, you have to be wise enough to address all possible nutritional deficiencies first before experimenting with your fast. Start with a solid nutritional platform if you are truly serious about doing intermittent fasting.

Also, remember that hunger is one of the major side effects of IF. It might also cause you to feel weak or lower the performance of your brain. Fortunately, these effects are usually only temporary. You will most likely experience them only while your body is still adapting to your new habits and eating patterns.

However, if you are suffering from a medical condition, seeking the advice of your doctor first is a must. Your doctor's opinion is even more important if you have diabetes, issues with regulating blood sugar, and low blood pressure.

Should You Give It a Try?

One great thing about intermittent fasting is that it boasts of an outstanding safety profile. Fasting for a while will not cause you any harm, provided you are well-nourished and healthy overall. Here are some criteria to consider:

- Your relationship with food is healthy.
- You are capable of controlling your eating habits after breaking the fast.
- Your mental sharpness and productivity are not affected by fasting.
- You have good health overall.
- You have low or manageable stress levels.

The best way to determine if intermittent fasting is good for you is to try it for a while. If you still feel great even when you are fasting, and you discover that this approach is a more sustainable eating solution for you, then you can view it as a truly powerful tool for your weight loss journey.

You can even use it to improve your health. Also, remember that there are certain factors that you have to focus on to maximize its benefits, including your workouts, sleeping patterns, and healthy eating habits.

What Body Type Can Benefit More from Intermittent Fasting?

As mentioned earlier, you can't expect intermittent fasting to work for everyone. The principles, patterns, and guidelines behind it do not suit all body types too. It should be noted that there are three basic body types. There is the mesomorph, which is characterized by a solid and strong build.

Those who have this body type are usually not underweight nor overweight. They seem to have rectangular body shapes and come with upright postures. Mesomorphs also have muscular legs and arms, muscular shoulders and chest, and even weight distribution.

Since mesomorphs do not often experience trouble eating whatever they want because they tend to lose weight easily, they may have an easier time crafting the perfect diet plan for them. However, they also tend to gain weight readily. In that case, intermittent fasting will surely work for them as this allows them to eat whatever they want during the eating window without worrying about their weight suddenly increasing.

Another body type that you have to be aware of is the endomorph. The endomorph body type is often characterized by fewer muscles and body fats. This is the reason why those with this body type usually look soft and round. They also tend to put on pounds quickly and easily.

However, take note that being an endomorph does not necessarily mean you are already overweight. It is just that this body type tends to gain more weight easily than the others. It is also quick and easy for endomorphs to increase their strength and build muscles.

If you have this body type, then a wise tip when it comes to dieting is to try reducing your carb intake. It is also advisable to increase your intake of water and other healthy beverages for proper hydration. It is also important to note that endomorphs respond better to intermittent fasting compared to the other body types.

With that in mind, it is no longer surprising to see IF being the go-to solution for endomorphs who are trying to lose weight or maintain a fit body. Intermittent fasting also seems to work more effectively for endomorphs based on their metabolic rate.

The last body type is an ectomorph. You can see ectomorphs having a thinner body and lower weight and longer limbs. Compared to endomorphs, ectomorphs have a more accelerated metabolism. It is also not easy for them to gain muscles, though it is necessary for them to perform certain exercises to improve their strength.

If you are an ectomorph, then know that your metabolism is different from endomorphs. In this case, intermittent fasting is not a good fit for your body type. It is the reason why it is not highly recommended for them. As far as body type is concerned, IF seems to work more suitably for endomorphs.

Chapter 9: Most Common Mistakes to Avoid
Common Mistakes

The concept of intermittent fasting seems fairly honest. You withhold from eating in intervals somewhere between 16 or 20 hours a day or heavily restrict your intake and eat a very low-calorie diet a couple of days a week. There are also some IF followers who eat just one meal a day (also called OMAD).

There's quite a bit of research proving that IF works for weight loss and improves things like blood sugar control and cholesterol, which are indicators for chronic diseases. Some studies have even found that IF may boost people's energy and help them sleep better.

There happens to be a lot of misinformation floating around the internet, so I culled a list of some of the top comments and questions and answered them the best I could. Here are some common questions I found about IF, plus some common faults to avoid when trying it.

Here are the top mistakes that I see people making all the time when they are fasting:

1. You're jumping into intermittent fasting too fast

The biggest reason most diets fail is because they're such an extreme departure from our common, natural way of eating that they often feel impossible to maintain. Just a thought, but if you're new to IF and are familiar to eating every two hours on the hour, maybe don't throw yourself into a hardcore 24-hour fast from hell.

If you're adamant about the concept of fasting, start with some beginners 12/12 method where you're fasting for 12 hours per day and eating within the 12-hour window. That's probably pretty close to what you're used to doing anyway, and who knows, it might be the only (if even that) defensible way to follow along.

2. You're choosing the wrong plan for your lifestyle

Again, don't set yourself up for misery by signing up for something you know is going to cramp your style. If you're a night owl, don't plan to start your fast at 6 p.m. If you're a daily gym-goer who Instagram's their WOD every morning and aren't willing to sacrifice your daily spin, don't choose a plan that severely restricts calories a few days a week.

3. You're eating too much during the eating window

This one is the most common trap I would expect to see people fall into with IF. If you've chosen a particularly obstructive regimen that's left you hungry for hours of the day, the moment the clock says "it's time to eat," you're likely to go a wee bit overboard. Research suggests restrictive diets often don't work because we tend to become so emotionally (and physically) starved that when we do allow ourselves to eat, we go hog wild and overeat in a fit of deprivation. Any diet that has you preoccupied with your next meal is a recipe for a binge so make sure you're not allowing yourself to feel unnecessarily hungry for long periods of time.

4. You're not eating enough during the eating window

Yep, not eating enough is also legit cause of weight gain, and I'll tell you why. In addition to setting yourself up for a rebound similar to what we deliberated with the last common IF mistake, not eating enough cannibalizes your muscle mass, causing your metabolism to slow.

Without that metabolic muscle mass, you may be sabotaging your ability to maintain (never mind to lose) fat in the future. The challenge with IF is that, because you're eating according to some arbitrary temporal rules, rather than listening to your body's innate cues, it's really difficult to know your true needs.

If you're adamant about doing the diet, be sure to speak to a registered dietitian to help you assess and meet your nutrient needs safely.

5. Using it as an excuse to eat rubbish

Unfortunately, people think that intermittent fasting is a magic pill that will solve all their problems. Yes, it is an incredibly effective tool to take control of your health but it won't cancel out eating a diet full of processed foods and sugar. When you are intermittent fasting it is even more important to nourish your body with nutrient dense, whole foods.

When you are in the fasted state, your body starts to break down damaged components and then uses them for of energy; this process cleans and heals the body. It also means your body becomes more sensitive to the food you eat, this is great if it's full of nutrients to nourish the body, but not good if you are eating rubbish.

Not only that, if you aren't nourishing yourself with nutrient dense foods, you will feel hungry all the time—your body will crave nutrients.

6. You're eating too many calories

"Does anyone else eat like crazy right when the fast is over and is it normal to have a huge appetite during the feeding period? It is hard for me to get full after a 20 hour fast and I just eat the whole 4 hours. LOL."

I'd venture to guess that this person is eating more calories than what's needed in that 4-hour window. So instead of laughing your way through a marathon all-you-can-eat session, plan for how you'll break your fast. Stock up on high-protein foods (like meats and seafood) and/or high-fiber foods (like fruits, vegetables, beans, and most whole grains). They'll not only fill you up, but will keep you feeling full.

"If I do a 20:4 fast then I should consume 1500-2000 calories within four hours? Do I understand this correctly?"

Technically, yes. But depending on a person's body size, eating 2,000 calories in a 4-hour window might not yield any weight loss. I don't know this person's size, though. Now, most people lose weight on 1,500 calories, but one of the pros of IF is that it's hard to eat a ton of calories in a short window of time.

For some, following IF is an easier way to cut calories and lose weight than simply following a traditional calorie-restricted diet. So if you can't hit the 1,500 or 2,000-calorie mark in 4 hours every day, it's OK. If falling below 1,200 calories a day becomes a regular habit, though, reconsider your diet plan. If you're not sure how many calories you're consuming, track them in a free app like MyFitnessPal.

7. You're overanalyzing

"Does IF mean no food outside meal times, or no calories?"

Um, they are one in the same, no? Does anyone reading this article know of foods that have zero calories? If so, please share! This person's assumption is correct, though—no food and no calories outside of the "feeding window."

Does anyone else feel like this question comes up about a thousand times a day? Short answer: Yes. Eating anything with calories breaks your fast.

Exceptions to this rule would be black coffee, unsweetened and milk-free tea, water, and diet soda (though research says diet soda could actually increase your appetite, which might make it hard to stick to your fast).

8. You're pushing yourself too hard

"I've been doing IF almost 2 months, mostly OMAD, sometimes 48/72 hours extended fasts. The last 3 or 4 days whenever I break my fast I feel a great regret. I always feel like I could push the fast a little longer. What should I do?"

Extending a fast doesn't supercharge the powers of IF. If this sounds familiar to you, please find yourself a counselor who specializes in eating disorders.

I'm not saying you, or this person here, has an eating disorder, but food should not induce feelings of remorse or regret. Left untreated, this could develop into a larger problem. And also, huge kudos to this person for so bravely speaking up and sharing their food feelings!

9. Attempting to do too many things at once—over train, under eat and try fasting

If you have spent a number of years eating badly and not exercising and you would like to try IF, don't bite off more than you can chew (pun intended!) at the start. Ease yourself into fasting and training gradually; don't start training five times per week fasting every day and restricting calories when you do eat from day one.

The combination can lead to problems. Your body thrives with a few physical stress here and there, but too much stress can create chronic issues.

10. You're not drinking enough

Your intermittent fasting regimen might have you refraining from food, but water should always be nearby, especially since you're missing out on the hydration you often get from foods like fruits and veggies. Dehydration can lead to muscle cramps, headaches, and exacerbate hunger pangs, so always make sure you're sipping H2O between (and during) feasts.

Followed all the rules and still struggling? It's not you; it's likely the diet. Research suggests that intermittent fasting has a 31 percent dropout rate, while research on diets in general suggests that as much as 95 percent of diets fail.

Try to focus more on what your body tells you, rather than what the clock says, and you're much more likely to get the nutrition your body needs.

11. Giving up too soon

Intermittent fasting takes a certain amount of discipline, but as mentioned above, it also takes time to get used to. The first four to five days are definitely the hardest. You will feel hungry.

You might feel lightheaded or exhausted or get headaches. Know that those feelings quickly pass and by the end of the first week, your body will start to adapt.

Your hunger will actually diminish and you'll start to feel more energetic and more focused. If you don't feel better after the first week, you may be doing too much too soon, or you may have chosen a plan that doesn't work for you.

How to Avoid Common Mistakes

Tip 1: Gradually stretch out the number of hours you go between meals until you reach a 12-hour eating window. Then move to a 10-hour eating window and reduce by small increments until you reach your goal.

Tip 2: Plan ahead. Prepare a healthy meal that's ready for you when your fast ends and make sure to eat whole ingredients when possible including healthy carbs like whole grains, lean protein, and plenty of veggies, says Fung.

Tip 3: Track your hydration using an app like MyFitnessPal, which can help keep you accountable and stick to water, plain tea, or black coffee while fasting.

Tip 4: "Gradually change your diet along with your eating schedule by incorporating healthier foods slowly," suggests Stephens. This prevents you from trying to overhaul everything at once, which is more sustainable.

Tip 5: Keep up with your usual workout routine or try something low-impact like walking. If you fast overnight and exercise in the morning, you can eat a protein-rich meal after, which helps you increase the rate at which you build muscle.

Tip 6: Shift your schedule forward or backward by a few hours on days when you've got plans with friends so you can still enjoy socializing. "It's a lifestyle, and it has to fit into life's special occasions," an expert says. "Intermittent fasting can be flexible."

Chapter 10: Frequently Asked Questions about Intermittent Fasting

How Long Will I Continue to Fast?
Did you know that there are many commonalities between this feeding system and how naturally slender people eat? Sometimes they eat, other times they just miss meals, that's how the nutrition is. If you become familiar with your selected IF schedule, your calorie intake will decrease until it becomes normal for you. You can change your frequency once you get the weight you need. It's best to keep fasting and not stop at all. It aims to permanently change your lifestyle, not just for a short time. It is a daily practice that guarantees consistent weight reduction.

I Take Some Medications Which Require Me to Eat, What Do I Do during the Fasting Times to Take Medicine?
You can experience some side effects when you take any medicines on an empty belly. Iron supplements can cause sickness and nausea; aspirin can cause stomach ulcers and upsets. It's better to ask the doctor if you should take this drug as you continue a fast. You can take medicine with small, low-calorie leafy vegetables that do not interfere with your pace. Your blood pressure can drop over the fasting period so that if you take blood pressure-lowering medicine, the blood pressure may become too low and lead to headaches.

What Food Is Better to Eat Raw or Cooked Vegetables?
There have been several discussions on this subject. Some argue that food preparation leads to vitamins, enzymes, and minerals destruction. But it also makes cellulose fiber more available for your system, among other nutrients. When prepared, carrots, fungi, spinach, chips, peppers, and other vegetables provide more antioxidants, but the disadvantage is that vitamin C may be lost when cooking. There is no official response; all you have to do is eat plenty of vegetables in whatever way you want.

I Am Old, Is It Too Late for Me to Start Fasting?
Starting fasting can never be too late. It can help you manage your appetite, help you lose weight, and even make your life longer. You'll quickly notice the impacts; you'll feel healthier, slimmer, and stronger. Start immediately.

When I take a treat like a packet of chips during my fasting period, what's going to happen?
Fasting is a seasonal activity involving voluntary meal abstinence. Not only does it help you, because you consume fewer calories, it's also because that's what your flesh was built to do. Do not equate fasting with starvation because starvation is bad, but fasting is good. IF's aim is to provide your body with free time to relax from food. Your improvement will end with just one snack, and your blood sugar levels will allow you to get out of a fasted state.

What Should I Do If I Don't Lose Weight?
Weight loss is a gradual process that takes quite some time to accomplish; thus, patient and consistency are needed. If you don't lose some weight in the first few weeks, you should just keep going, and you shouldn't be concerned. It's important to keep track of the food you eat so you can track the problem easily.

During My Period, Is It Really Safe to Fast?
Fasting is not at all right when you are pregnant or breastfeeding, but your monthly cycles will not affect your fast in any way unless they are very painful or intolerable. If so, you can test your iron levels and take supplements as well.

I Have Diabetes, Can I Still Practice IF?
If you have type 1 or type 2 diabetes or on diabetes medication, you need to take additional care while practicing IF. If the need arises, your doctor will check your blood sugar levels carefully to change your medicine prescription to allow them to co-exist with intermittent fasting peacefully. When you can't be closely monitored, don't attempt fasting. It decreases the blood sugar levels and continuing to take drugs as insulin can lead to exceptionally low concentrations of blood glucose that lead to hypoglycemia. You can drink a sugar-filled drink like soda and even stay off your fasting routine one day to raise the level of blood sugar. If you have blood sugar levels that are excessively low, this is due to over-medication and not intermittent fasting. Reduce your use of medications in advance because you expect lower levels of blood sugar when you begin IF.

Is It True That I Can Eat All I Want on Non-fast Days?
This is true as all foods are allowed. It is permissible to use anything from the most oil-drenched fried chicken to a vegetable salad for any other meat. It is best not to consume too much as if during the time you were fasting, you are struggling to eat what you would have. You may even overcome the impacts of fasting when you overfeed. It should not be made into a ritual of overeating after fasting; eating should be done responsibly. But it all boils down to what you want to do, as you are the one that decides to fast and by now you already know a lot of the do and don't. You'll automatically find yourself choosing healthier meals after doing the fasting for some time.

Can I Get Tired from Fasting, If So, How Could I Stop It?
No, the opposite would actually happen. Individuals have more strength in fasting as a result of higher levels of adrenaline in the body. With more than enough energy, you will certainly be able to conduct your ordinary operations. Fatigue is not a normal part of fasting, so if you feel exhausted, stop fasting right away and see a doctor right away.

Can I Receive the Same Benefits of Fasting as an Adult of the Opposite Sex?
Hormonally and metabolically, there are several differences between men and women. For example, women store more fat and are more susceptible to exercise-dependent fat burning. Research has shown that fasting females respond more quickly to endurance exercise, while fasting males react more quickly with a weighted workout. IF's benefits on both genders are almost equal. It's not supposed to be a race, but more of individual experience, so concentrating on your body is better than thinking about others.

During the First Days of Fasting, I Want to Use Meal Replacement Shakes, Is It All Right or Should I Just Stick to Food?
During the first days of IF training, these meal replacement shakes have helped most individuals. These are definitely better than calorie counting, as you can just sip free from your thirst. Even if the real nutrition is considered to be more effective when you like these drinks, you can go ahead and use them. Make sure that you only have those that have small or even no glucose.

Can I Get the Intermittent Fasting Result in Me Getting Headaches?
Sure, but it only happens due to fatigue and not due to low calories. You may have withdrawal symptoms, but they are gentle. Make sure you take medication on an ongoing basis to treat the migraine as you would a normal one. If during the fasting period, you feel ill, you must stop immediately.

If I Observe Intermittent Fasting, What Amount of Weight Can I Lose?
That's based on a number of factors and variations between individuals. Such factors are like your heart rate, your exercise level, and how closely you observe the pace. During the first week, you will lose water, and you will eventually lose weight as a result of your daily calorie intake. It's not advised to lose really fast weight and shouldn't be an aim; it's better to lose a little weight continuously.

Could I Easily Get Cranky as I Practice IF?
It has been used in all hundreds of years; this has never been an issue; it is not even in societies that have fasting as an essential part of their beliefs. Moreover, Buddhist monks are considered to be very peaceful people while they practically fast daily; fasting has no such effect.

I Happen to Be Naturally Slender; Thus, I Don't Require Any Weight Loss, Can I Still Practice IF for Its Physiological Benefits?
If you're comfortable with your weight, that's fine, and fasting is very much still an option you have to improve your health. You have to make sure that during your feeding time, you focus more on calorie-dense meals—most slender people who fast get all the advantages without any problem. Testing through trial and error is the only way you can find the right balance between eating and fasting to keep you at a safe weight. Reduce the days of fasting by constantly checking your weight and take care not to get underweight as that would be hazardous to you.

Can I Get Too Much Food as a Result of Fasting?
The answer is yes and no to this question. First, it's really because you're going to consume more than you usually do after fasting. It is not, however, since feeding above the regular amounts in no days of fasting is not a consequence of fasting.

I'm Going to Sleep Hungry When My Fasting Time Is at Night?
It's not probable, but it's mainly dependent on your metabolism, just try to keep your mind away from food and feel hungry. When you get out of your bed, you may not feel hungry at all. Essentially, your appetite and hunger will suit your fasting routine.

Can IF Make My Body Go into Starvation Mode to Prevent More Loss of Fat?
This is not a realistic side effect because there is no calorie restriction on IF. There's no IF routine that's intense to the point you're going into starvation mode. The fasting time is short, so from the fat stores, the body absorbs fat and retains muscle mass. Research has shown that IF does not lower any individual's metabolic rate. Despite long fasts like those for three days, there will be no decrease in the basal metabolic rate. There is also no increase in the hunger hormone called ghrelin during IF.

I'm an Overweight Fellow, Is IF Really the Key to Solving My Problem?
Intermittent fasting has proved to be one of the most effective and enduring strategies for obese individuals to lose and retain new weight. The bigger you are, the greater the initial loss of weight. You've most likely given up conventional restrictive diets. Intermittent fasting has an advantage over all of them because it is more versatile, and when you consume anything, it is not a crime because nothing is restricted. Research has shown that obese individuals are very easily used to fasting.

Can I Eat during My Fasting Time If I Really Have to, like during Celebrations and Major Ceremonies?
Be active, but concentrate on what you're ingesting. While it's vital to get help from your family and friends, if you keep telling them you can't eat as you are in a fast, they'll start to get tired of hearing that, and eventually you'll feel self-conscious. This will render it an obstacle to your normal activity, which is not its original intent, rather than something that fits perfectly in your life. When you know that there is a social event connected to food, then fast the day before or the day before. It is a very flexible device, and without any difficulties, you will continue to be active and enjoy these times.

Chapter 11: The Right Mindset When Starting IF

When setting out on your intermittent fasting journey, it's important to keep in mind that success is built on several good practices.

The best part is that these secrets are really easy to implement into your routine. So, don't be afraid to give them a try.

The Difference between Needing and Wanting to Eat

It is of the utmost importance for you to recognize when you are really hungry and when you think you are hungry.

There Is A Huge Difference Here

Often, we fall into the trap of eating without actually being hungry. If you are guilty of this, it's time that you started noticing what triggers these cravings. For instance, if you overeat when you are anxious, then it might be a good idea for you to pay close attention to these instances. That can make a significant difference in your overall success.

Eat Only When Needed

When you are able to recognize when you eat without being hungry, you begin to create a discipline in which you eat only when needed. The easiest way to do this is to build a schedule and then stick to it. Building a rather strict schedule will help you accustom your body to eating only when really needed. This approach will go a long way in helping you stretch your fasting periods.

Hydration Is Essential

Throughout this book, we've talked about how essential it is to hydrate during fast days. You need to make sure that you drink plenty of water. While plain water is perfectly healthy, it should also be mentioned that fruit and vegetable juices are a great source of nutrition.

Ideally, you would consume these juices without any added sugar. Generally speaking, most fruits and vegetables have very little calories. So, you won't blow your calorie budget during fast days. Moreover, most fruits don't have a high glucose content. For instance, apples and lemons don't have much glucose. However, oranges and bananas do. Thus, you want to stick to apple juice and lemon water while cutting down a bit on orange juice. If you can get fresh oranges and squeeze them, you could build a winning formula without consuming needless sugar.

Take Things Slowly

To make this easier, you could use the following rule of thumb. If you are planning to fast on a Monday, you could ramp down your meals, starting with Sunday's lunch. For example, a wholesome lunch (not overdoing it) followed by a very light dinner roughly two hours before bedtime will help you set yourself up for success. Then, consume plenty of water upon getting up on Monday morning. This will keep you full throughout the early morning. Next, make a plan to consume some fruit or non-fat, unsweetened yogurt. This should give you the caloric intake you need. Assuming you are doing a 12-hour fast, plan to have a very light lunch. That way, you won't be burdening your digestive system following the fast. Lastly, you can have a normal dinner, but without overdoing it. The next day, you can go about your usual eating habits.

With this approach, you will never go wrong. You will always feel comfortable at all times during your fasting days.

Cut down on Carbs and Sugar Even on Non-fast Days

During non-fast days, you are free to have your usual eating regimen. However, it's best to cut down on sugar and carbs since being hooked on these will make it very difficult for you to get through a fasting period. In fact, folks who try to fast while seriously hooked on sugar and carbs often feel anxious and edgy. They even suffer from mild to serious withdrawal symptoms.

So, the best way to go about it is to cut down on your sugar intake well before attempting to go on a full fast. For instance, you can cut down on your portion sizes roughly two weeks before attempting to do your first fast. That way, you can begin the detoxing process while avoiding any nasty withdrawal symptoms.

Keep Track of Your Achievements

We're going old school here. Keep track of your achievements by using a regular notebook. There is something about writing things down on paper that makes it highly personal. When you do this, you can see how you have been progressing. Make sure to write down the date and the length of each fast. Also, include some notes about the things that went right and the things that didn't go right. That way, you can see how your intermittent fasting regimen has been affecting you both positively and negatively.

Over time, you can look back to see the progress you have made. This is why journaling can be one of the most important things that you can do to give yourself the boost you need, especially when you are feeling down. We don't recommend using note-taking or journaling apps on your phone or tablet as they tend to be rather impersonal. Additionally, a notebook or diary is a very personal item. Please bear in mind that this is a very personal journey. As a result, chronicling your achievements will enable you to keep things closer to heart.

Chapter 12: The Basics of Intermittent Fasting
Must-Follow Guidelines

1. Chart your progress
Make a plan and write it down. Keeping a diary is useful to see if this diet is working for you. Data shows that dieters who write daily notes are more successful at losing weight with intermittent fasting.

2. Prep
Prep your fast-day food in advance. This will help you to maintain the keto diet and intermittent fasting combination.

3. Breaking your fast
Break your fast with a snack. Often we overeat as soon as the fast is over. We eat more because of a psychological need. Not because of hunger. When your fast is over, eat a small snack or a small dish, then wait for 30 minutes to an hour then eat your main meal. This will help you to avoid overeating. Here are some suggestions for your first snack when you break your fast:
1. A small bowl of soup
2. A small amount of meat
3. A small bowl of raw vegetables
4. A small salad
5. 1/3 cup nuts
6. Avoid suppressing

Don't try to suppress your thoughts of food during your fast. It is because of a psychological mechanism called habituation. If you have something in abundance, then you put less value on it. So trying to suppress the thought of food during your fast is the wrong strategy. Do not try to associate fasting with discomfort.

5. Stay hydrated
Drink plenty of water. Remember, a dry mouth is a sign of dehydration, so act before your body complains. Drink approximately eight big glasses of water. Drinking water will help you to suppress your hunger.

6. Weight loss
How much weight you will lose depends on your body type, your activity level, your starting weight, your metabolism, and how much you consume during your non-fast days.

If you are not losing weight:
- Be patient. Some people need a longer time to lose weight.
- Be realistic. The average weight loss is more likely to be around 1 to 2 pounds per week.
- Avoid binging.
- Keep a food diary.

- Look at the calories you are receiving from fizzy drinks, smoothies, alcohol, juices, lattes, and drinks.
- Try adding more fast days

7. Is breakfast vital?
Often, people say that breakfast is vital. However, a study concluded that both breakfast eaters and skippers lost the same amount of weight.

8. Drinks during no fast days
Drink lots of water. Use lemon, mint leaves, cloves, ginger, and lemongrass to flavor your water. Drink herbal teas such as lavender, chamomile, rose, ginger, cinnamon, lemongrass, and licorice.

9. Supplements
You do not need any supplements, but if you are fond of supplements, then here are a few that you can take during your fast days:
- **Glucosamine**—ideal for relieving joint pain.
- **Casein Protein**—ideal for pre-bedtime.
- **Whey Protein**—protein boost for pre and post-workout.
- **Beta-Alanine**—boosts exercise performance.
- **Branched Chain Amino Acids (BCAA)**—can help limit lean body mass loss as well as increasing visceral fat loss.
- **Vitamin D**—helps you function optimally.
- **Calcium**—increases fast excretion and boosts testosterone.
- **Fish Oil**—helps keep your omega-3 and 6 levels up.
- **Multivitamin**—to overcome any deficiencies you may have.

10. Gender differences
Men and women have metabolic and hormonal differences. They store and utilize fat in different ways. Fasting aids both sexes, and studies show positive results.
However, fasting is not meant to be a struggle, so be cautious and self-aware. Listen to your body.

11. Fasting during menstruation
Some women may find fasting more challenging in the days preceding a period. If you feel any discomfort, then avoid fasting during your period.

12. When trying to conceive
The science is still unfolding, but health experts say an intermittent fasting plan will not affect fertility. But more extreme fasting may (such as the 36-hour fast). Be cautious and avoid fasting when you are trying to get pregnant.

13. If you have headaches
Headaches occur due to dehydration rather than fasting itself. Drink plenty of water during your fast.

14. Constipation
It can happen if you have too much fiber in your diet.

15. Affecting sleep
Some people find it difficult to go to bed hungry. Drink a glass of milk or eat a small snack before bed.

16. Time-frame
Do not fast for more than 36 hours. Fasting for a long time will trigger various negative symptoms that you want to avoid. If you fast for too long, you will start to lose muscle and protein tissue instead of fat. You want to lose fat to lose weight. Losing too much muscle will make you unhealthy.

17. Do not rush
If you have a certain health condition, then do not rush into fasting. Discuss with your doctor before starting intermittent fasting.

Health Concerns

1. Muscle cramps
Low magnesium can cause muscle cramps. Take an over-the-counter magnesium supplement, or you can apply magnesium oil on your skin.

2. Heartburn
Do not eat a large meal when you break your fast. It might cause heartburn. Drinking sparkling water with lemon often helps.

3. Constipation
Increase your intake of fiber, vegetables, and fruits during your non-fasting days to prevent constipation.

4. Dizziness
Consume normal levels of salt and water daily to cure dizziness. Also, low blood pressure may be a cause of dizziness.

Chapter 13: Basic of Eating on Intermittent Fasting
Which Type of Food?

1. Do Not Be Afraid To Think About Your Favorite Food
The psychological mechanism called "getting used"—the more people have something, the less they are tied to it—doing the opposite and trying to suppress food thinking is a faulty strategy. Does that mean...? Treat food as friends, not as enemies. Eating is not magical, supernatural, or dangerous. Do not make it the hell. Normalize it. Just eat.

2. Add Water
Find a non-calorie drink that you like, and then swallow it in bulk. Some people swear by herbal tea. Others prefer foamy mineral water to dance on their tongues, but also tap water. Much of our hydration comes from the foods we eat. Therefore, we may need to add additional drinks beyond our usual intake (check your urine, your urine is pale enough; should be). There is no scientific basis for drinking the recommended eight glasses of water a day. Still, there are good reasons to continue drinking. A dry mouth is the last, but not the first sign of dehydration. So, act and recognize before your body is dissatisfied. A glass of water is a quick way to stop hunger, at least temporarily. Also, you will no longer confuse your thirst with hunger.

3. Do Not Expect Weight Loss on Any Particular Day
If you have a week where your scale does not seem to shift, even if you do not see the numbers falling, consider the health benefits you will get instead. Remember why you are doing this; not only smaller jeans but also the long-term benefits, the generally accepted advantage of intermittent fasting, destroys diseases, and strengthens the brain. Extend life. Think of it as your body's pension fund.

4. Be Wise, Be Careful, and Stop If You Feel Wrong
This strategy must be implemented flexibly and tolerantly. You can break the rules if you need to. It is not a race to the finish. So be kind to you and be entertaining. Who wants to live longer when life is miserable? You do not want to growl or sweat in a tired life. You want to go dancing, right?

5. Congratulations
A complete fasting day implies potential weight loss and quantifiable health gains. You have already won. Is breakfast important?
The diet tradition has long indicated that breakfast is the most important meal of the day. Missing it in the morning is like leaving your house without a coat. But not always. According to a recent survey, the more breakfast you have, the bigger your lunch (and dinner). This is not surprising, but it does increase the total number of calories for the day. Wait for a quick later. It is up to you, and the pattern you choose may change over time.

Which Type of Fluid?
Plenty—unless it has actual calorie content. In fact, as with most decisions on a fast diet, the choice is entirely up to you. Drink plenty of water—it is calorie-free, actually free, fuller than you think, and avoids upsetting your thirst because of hunger. In summer, add a round of cucumber or a pinch of lime. Freeze it and smoke the cube. If you want warmth, miso soup is protein-rich, feels like food, and consumes only 84 calories per cup. Vegetable soup does the same trick. If you are having trouble sleeping, one low-calorie hot chocolate can contain less than 40 calories and can calm you down. Calorie-free drinks are best during the day. It is recommended to pour hot water with lemon to get your digestive system moving. However, it is recommended to add a pinch of mint leaves or cloves, ginger root slices, or lemongrass. If you like herbal teas, try the unusual flavors (licorice and cinnamon, lemongrass and ginger, lavender, rose, and chamomile). Green tea can have good antioxidant properties. Yes, there is no jury. Please drink if you like it. Black sugar-free tea and coffee on fasting days can be taken. It is okay if you like milk and artificial sweeteners. But remember that milk calories are added. You are trying to extend the time when you are not burning calories.
Fruit juices look healthy, but are generally surprisingly sugary, contain less fiber than whole fruits, and can increase stealth calories without leaving leaves. Commercial smoothies can have a sugar content similar to that of cola. Because they are acidic, they erode the teeth. They are also loaded with calories. If you want a taste, replace the juice and smoothie with very lean liquor. Probably a dash of elderflower with gushing water and lots of ice.

How about Alcohol?
Alcoholic drinks are comfortable, but they only offer "empty" calories. A glass of white wine contains about 120, while a can of 550 ml of beer contains 250. If you cannot say no, skip these on fasting days. This is a unique opportunity to reduce your weekly consumption without continuously feeling disadvantaged. Think of it as an alcoholic two days a week.

And Caffeine?
There is growing evidence that drinking coffee far away from guilty pleasure is useful for preventing mental decline, improving heart health, and reducing the risk of liver cancer and stroke. So, if it moves you and keeps you moving every day, keep drinking coffee. It is a useful weapon against boredom in your arsenal, and coffee breaks can comfortably interrupt your day. There is no metabolic reason to avoid caffeine during the fast. However, if you have problems sleeping, limit your intake later in the day. Of course, please drink black. Chocolates not allowed.
Did you know that chocolate bars are hardly organic food, but did you know what a sweet mocha or apple bar can be? Although processed foods tend to have hidden sugars, which are practical, they do not have the nutritional benefits of useful old plants and proteins. Try carrots, celery sticks, hummus, or a few nuts. Always count them in your daily calories (do not cheat).
Even low-calorie, nutritious foods, and frequent snacks are not recommended. Do not overstimulate as this is part of the motivation to exercise your appetite. If your

mouth desperately needs attention, give it a drink. Is it possible to get past the early days using a meal exchange?

Shake/Juice?

Many people say that over-the-counter dietary supplement shakes helped them through the first, usually the hardest, week of intermittent fasting. Shaking is probably easier than counting calories, and on a hungry day, you can take a sip when the hungry waves hit. We aren't big fans because we think real food is better. But if you find it useful, definitely try it. It is best to choose a brand with low sugar content. What are the consequences of fraud and some chips or cookies?

For clarity, this is a book about fasting and voluntary abstention from eating. The reason why this is good for you goes far beyond the fact that you simply eat fewer calories. It occurs because our body is designed for intermittent fasting. Adversity only makes you stronger. While hunger is terrible; some little short, sharp, and shocking food restrictions are reasonable.

Your goal is, therefore, to open a food-free breathing space for your body. It does not hurt to reach 510 calories (615 calories for men). Fasting never goes away. The idea of reducing calories by a quarter of your daily intake on a day of fasting has only been clinically proven to have a systemic effect on metabolism. There is no particular "magic" at 500 or 600 calories, but you should stick to these numbers. Specific parameters are required to make a strategy effective in the medium term. An "extra cookie" on a fasting day is precisely the opposite of your goal (which will likely increase your blood sugar and consume most of your tolerated amount in a butter bite). Needless to say, if you are fasting, you need to think wisely and consistently about your food choices according to the plan outlined here. "I will be motivated to exercise, and I will remember that tomorrow is approaching."

Who Else Should Not Fast?

There are certain groups where fasting is not recommended. People with type 1 diabetes and people with eating disorders are included. If you are already very slim, do not fast. Children should never fast. They are still growing and should not be exposed to any nutritional stress. If you have an underlying disorder, talk to your doctor about how to do it before starting to lose weight.

Chapter 14: How to Practice: Step-by-Step Guide to Intermittent Fasting

A Weekly Meal Plan Template

Some days are blocked off. These days can be edited depending on the method you will be using.

Day	Breakfast	Lunch	Dinner	Snack
Day 1				
Day 2				
Day 3				
Day 4				
Day 5				
Day 6				
Day 7				

30 Day Workout Plan Using 16/8

Week 1

In the first week, you'll only conform with the window.

Tasks

1. Choose your favorite eating window for eight hours. Note that your fasting time is dedicated to sleep. Try to base the feeding period on moments where you know it's going to be difficult not to feed and exercise.
2. Don't dramatically change the type of food you eat. It's about getting used to the food window this week.
3. Do not attempt exercise if you are new to the practice of fasting; the most probable surge in appetite may find restraint more challenging. Only focus on sitting in your room.
4. Practice Monday-Friday's 16:8 approach and have the weekend off.

Week 2

If you were able to stick to the tasks outlined in week 1, then continue to the tasks listed below. We're going to address sleep this week and start the 16:8 food pattern.

Tasks

1. Assess the feeding period for the last weeks. You've got to change it? Is it by your schedule? If so, start Monday-Friday to use this opportunity. If no, select a new period for feeding and replicate week 1.
2. Implement one of the four suggestions outlined earlier in this book, Monday-Friday for better sleep. If you have itchy feet, feel free to exercise gently! Nonetheless, if you are dealing with a hunger to enable your feeding period to be fully adapted, I would still suggest no workout.
3. Also, don't radically change the type of food you eat.

Week 3

We're going to add exercise this week. You probably hanged out to blow some calories if you haven't begun already.

Tasks

1. Open the nutritional slot. Does this still work? Must it alter to make you more disciplined? Start with your current window Monday-Friday, if the window is perfect. If not, choose a new window and go back to week 1.
2. Depending on your ability level, incorporate sufficient HITT instruction. Using the HITT preparation tips described in this book earlier, build a two-three-fold exercise this week. Remember, please check with a qualified doctor before implementing every food or exercise plan.
3. Start to cut back on sugar. This task varies from person to person.

Week 4

You should have the ideal eating period in position by week four. If you are still suffering, I strongly suggest that you get a group that's assistance in week 3.

Tasks

1. Continue eating the time you have selected Monday-Friday
2. Add some of the foods listed for adding magnesium and potassium
3. Under electrolytes. Find choices for balanced dessert to help you stay happy! Here, the trick is to find keto desserts because they are high in fat and weak in carbohydrates. Keep in mind the fat spikes less insulin and makes the body turn to energy storage. Don't buy the policy of "low fat"
4. Implement a second tip outlined in this book for better sleep. (My favorite person is more sunlight)
5. Continue to remove sugar
6. Conduct 2-4 HITT exercises

The first 30 days of 16:8, as you can see, are not drastic. I didn't describe giving up pasta, potatoes, or even sweet treats. To keep you inspired to start, you will invest your first 30 days, making improvements and getting great results. How to get going is the key to long-term success. While I know how hungry you are for success, I caution against pushing forward as a novice. First of all, the number one reason people give up is for seeking too much, too fast. Sometimes we've been overweight or unhealthy for 5-20 years. In the blink of an eye, it is unrealistic to expect long life patterns and a lack of discipline to be changed.

Chapter 15: Best Exercises for Women above 50

The women above fifties have a hard time taking care of their bodies if they aren't active. Our body is unhealthy if it is subjected too long to a sedimentary lifestyle. There are multiple reasons for it. Some of the most active women I have seen in their fifties moved around their bodies quite a lot. They exercised their bodies, easily staying fit even when they aged. There were also cases of women who were only forty-five, but they had the problems of sixty-five years older women. I expected as much as seeing their sedimentary lifestyle. The exercise makes a hell lot of difference.

When you move around your body, you automatically push your body to regulate its functions, performing well. The body needs exercise just as our functions need to perform well. Exercise is the biggest difference-maker. It is that healthy habit that decides if you will automatically have a body of thirty years old while remaining fifty or have a body of sixty-five years old while remaining forty.

Generally, there are two kinds of females. The first type of females includes those ladies who have remained active in their youth. When they were in their twenties or thirties even, they moved around quite a lot. Yoga, jogging, and aerobics is something known to them. Naturally, they are also women who can do intermittent fasting better. Even if you are a woman in your fifties, you will remain much fitter if you exercised in your prime years.

There is another type of female who has led to a sedimentary lifestyle. Those females are often inactive, lacking any interest in exercise or physical activity. Often, the busy routine, along with the field of work, make this thing possible.

I can give you a piece of good news. Females who have not exercised in their twenties or even thirties can still reap the benefits of exercise. As you do intermittent fasting, you will realize that your bodies are more mobile than before, easily being able to do things you didn't think were possible. Even if you were a female who had led a life of physical inactiveness, you still have a shot at it. The intermittent fasting naturally reduces cholesterol, leading to a free and active body. For the females who had been quite active before and still do a tremendous amount of exercise, I would suggest cutting down a bit. Intermittent fasting combined with exercise is somewhat a powerful combo for weight loss and cholesterol reduction. However, you must avoid exhaustion. I will give a list of best exercises that are well suited for the women above fifties. You can choose a suitable time for these exercises, like in the morning or evening. Make sure to never overexert your body. Your body is your temple, and the more you take care of it, the more it will take care of you.

1. Walking/Jogging

This exercise is for the females who have led an inactive lifestyle. You can start with a thirty-minute walk in the park or even your home. Gradually increase it to forty-five minutes if possible. Walking is an amazing exercise if practiced daily. It is also the most basic form of exercise, leading females into a sense of activity. Interestingly, it is also preferred by women who were once very active but now have gone inactive physically. The best thing about walking is that it can be done in your street or even rooftop.

An advanced form of walking is jogging. You can try it out in the park. When you start walking and then gradually move towards jogging, there are a lot of benefits you will reap. Not only will your physical body be more active, but your mental health will also benefit from it.

2. Light Aerobics

Haven't you got much time? Or perhaps walking across the street or park is not possible? Light aerobics might just be what you need. You can start with light aerobics or low impact aerobics. There are a lot of YouTube videos available online. You can take a start from there. You will only need to do them 20 minutes a day for three to four days per week. The best thing about aerobics is that it easily provides an amazing exercise in a very short time. It doesn't require any equipment. All you need is a laptop to watch videos about them and space like a room. Don't exert too much pressure on your body. The fellows in the videos are experts. You just have to do the exercise and move your body.

3. Stretching/Yoga

The stretching exercises are naturally the best ones. You can easily do yoga for adults on an everyday basis. The best results come when you pair it with light aerobics or walking. Yoga or stretching exercises have immense benefits. They relieve joint pain, provide your bones strength and flexibility, and increase your immunity. The stretching exercises also allow your body to be more flexible and strong. Other than that, your mind will be relaxed as your body does the stretching. Yoga poses for adult women are easily available online. The same rule with light aerobics goes here too. You will need to take it easy and slow. Only stretch your body until a mild discomfort. Don't push too hard.

A yoga routine is easily available. If you are someone who hasn't exercised for years, then yoga is for you too. Naturally, the best duo I have seen in some females was doing mild yoga in the morning and pairing it with light aerobics or walking in the evening.

In case you do the intermittent fasting, even simple yoga might be enough.

4. Balance

There are plenty of light exercises that focus on improving your balance. Naturally, some poses of yoga also focus on balance. It is somewhat a crucial part of your health. You should focus on it quite often.

Chapter 16: Tips and Tricks for Staying Healthy

Once you get started with intermittent fasting, you will soon notice a natural tendency towards a more generally healthy lifestyle. This is a quite common virtuous circle; you start with a single healthy choice, this makes you feel better, and feeling better gives you the energy to go on with more healthy choices, in a snowball effect of wellness.

You will naturally know and feel what healthy changes you'll need to put into your life, and this will probably not only concern the body's health, but mind and spirit too.

So, now we are going to look at some aspects you should consider as a general lifestyle background for your intermittent fasting path; still, this is just some advice, please listen to yourself and be ready to embrace your body, mind, and spirit suggestions.

Moderate, If You Don't Want to Get Rid of Alcohol

In any case, alcohol may aggravate inflammation, limiting the benefits of the diet you are trying to achieve. Chronic inflammation such as heart disease, type 2 diabetes, and certain malignancies may advance different diseases. The intake of alcohol can likewise strain your liver, diminishing its capacity to sift through possibly damaging elements. Organ harm may be the result caused by the inflammation of the whole body that are consequences for your intestine and liver. Over the top, alcohol intake can cause far-reaching inflammation of the body, slowing if not stopping the effects of your diet and conceivably prompting infections.

Also, consider that drinking alcohol can break your intermittent fasting. When fasting, you should avoid foods and drinks for some time. In particular, intermittent fasting is intended to advance hormonal and physical changes—for example, fat consumption and cell repair. Apart from that, it is perfectly acceptable to drink in moderation during your eating periods.

During fasting periods, your body starts cell repair processes like autophagy, in which old, harmed proteins are expelled from cells to produce more effective, healthier cells. This process may diminish your danger of malignancy, distances the issues of aging effects, and at any rate, somewhat clarifies why calorie limitation has been shown to expand life expectancy. Ongoing animal studies show that constant alcohol intake may hinder autophagy in the liver and fat tissue.

Picking Better Alcohol Choices

As alcohol breaks your fast whenever expended during a fasting period, it is recommended to just drinking during your planned eating periods. You should likewise hold your intake under tight restraints. Moderate alcohol consumption is characterized as close to one drink a day for women and close to two a day for men. While intermittent fasting does not have exacting standards for food and drink intake, some alcohol habits are healthier than others and are more reluctant to hinder your dietary routine.

To restrict your sugar and calorie intake, avoid cocktails, and prefer wines. During intermittent fasting, it is ideal for drinking alcohol moderately and only during your eating windows.

The Unhindered Eating Trap
Anyone who has ever changed their diet to get a health benefit or a healthy weight realizes that you begin to desire foods that you are recommended not to eat. Truth be told, a study published in 2017 affirmed that an increased drive to eat is a key factor during a weight loss journey.
Nevertheless, this test is explicitly restricted on an intermittent fasting plan. Food limitation just happens during certain restricted hours, and on the non-fasting hours or days of the plan, you can, for the most part, eat anything you desire.
Keeping on with unhealthy foods may not be the healthiest way to pick up benefits from intermittent fasting; however, removing them during specific days restricts your overall intake and may, in the end, give benefits anyway.

Don't Stop Working Out
Or start doing it if you didn't.
You don't need to be an athlete, but you can't afford a sedentary lifestyle. Some people may think that since they are fasting, they should save energy and rest a lot. Well, that's not exactly like this. You should exercise as much as you can (that could be a little, for you, but still), just taking some care.
You should choose whether you would want to work out while fasting or after having eaten. On the chance that you stick to the early afternoon to 8 P.M. eating plan, this mainly comes down to whether you usually work out in the first part of the day or the evening. Remember that you can change your timetable to your necessities. If you want to work out toward the beginning of the day after eating, you can change your fasting and eating periods to do it.

Training during Fasting
Training in a fasted state requires a few supplements to keep your body in an anabolic state. The body utilizes amino acids for energy if you are training without a pre-exercise meal. Your supplements for fast ought to include glutamine and branched-chain amino acid (BCAA) supplement.
Following the early afternoon to 8 P.M. feeding plan, you fast from 8 P.M. until around noon. So, take your glutamine and BCAA enhancements, and then do your workout. Depending on how long your workout will last, this will set your post-exercise meal around the early afternoon.
What number of meals you decide to have during your starting period is up to you, however, remember that eating less as often as possible can hold your yearning within proper limits and support your body's capacity to build muscle.

Training during the Feeding Period
On the chance that you like to work out after eating, you can plan your exercise to fall in the afternoon (early around 1 P.M., or toward the evening, around 5 P.M.). If your workout session is for the most part in the late afternoon, have your pre-training meal around the early afternoon, work out, and afterward have your other meals.
For an evening session, have your first meal around early afternoon and your pre-exercise meal around 4 P.M. If you want to have a post-training meal one hour after working out, you can do that too.

Adjusting Your Calorie Intake

The main principles about intermittent fasting include a few directions of when and how to get your calories and macronutrients.

If you train while fasting, the calorie check of your BCAA supplement should be calculated toward your complete calories of the day, even though it does not end your fasting period. People on intermittent fasting plans normally distribute fifty calories for their fasting period to take into account things like supplements or refreshments. This implies you can, in any case, take cream and sugar in your espresso or tea, regardless of whether or not it is during your fasting period.

In case you eat a pre-training meal, it is preferable to keep it light. Your meal should include a protein source like poultry or fish and some carbs, for a total amount of 400-500 calories. This will give you the protein and complex starches that are often suggested for pre-exercise meals. If you do eat a pre-exercise meal, the BCAA supplements prescribed for fasting exercises are most likely redundant, but you might need to take them in any case, since having an overflow of BCAAs may now be helpful anyway.

Your post-training meal is the best time to take a large portion of your sugars and calories. About a big part of your total calories for the day ought to be eaten during your post-training meal.

Chapter 17: Recipes
Breakfast

#1 Avocado Egg Bowls
Preparation Time: 5 minutes
Cooking Time: 10 minutes
Servings: 3
Ingredients:
- 1 tsp. coconut oil
- 2 organics, free-range
- Salt and pepper
- 1 Large & ripe avocado

For Garnishing:
- Chopped walnuts
- Balsamic Pearls
- Fresh thyme

Directions:
1. Slice your avocado in two, then take out the pit and remove enough of the inside so that there is enough space inside to accommodate an entire egg.
2. Cut off a little bit of the bottom of the avocado so that the avocado will sit upright as you place it on a stable surface.
3. Open your eggs and put each of the yolks in a separate bowl or container. Place the egg whites in the same small bowl. Sprinkle some pepper and salt to the whites, according to your taste, then mix them well.
4. Melt the coconut oil in a pan that has a lid that fits and put it on med-high.
5. Put in the avocado boats, with the meaty side down on the pan, the skin side up and sauté them for approx. 35 seconds or when they become darker in color.
6. Turn them over, then add to the spaces inside, almost filling the inside with the whites of the eggs.
7. Then, reduce the temperature and place the lid. Let them sit covered it for approx. 16 to 20 minutes until the whites are just about fully cooked.
8. Gently add one yolk onto each of the avocados and keep cooking them for 4 to 5 minutes, just until they get to the point of cook you want them at.
9. Move the avocados to a dish and add toppings to each of them using the walnuts, the balsamic pearls, or/and thyme.

Nutrition:
- Calories: 215 kcal
- Total Fat: 18g
- Carbohydrates: 8g
- Protein: 9g

#2 Buttery Date Pancakes

Preparation Time: 10 minutes
Cooking Time: 10 minutes
Servings: 3

Ingredients:
- 1/4 cup almond flour
- 3 eggs, beaten
- 1 tsp. olive oil
- 6 dates, pitted
- 1 tbsp. almond butter
- 1 tsp. vanilla extract
- 1/2 tsp. ground cinnamon

Directions:
1. Stir the eggs in a bowl make them fluffy.
2. Wash the dates and cut them in half.
3. Discard the seeds and mash them finely.
4. Melt the almond butter and add to the eggs.
5. Add the almond flour, olive oil, and cinnamon.
6. Mix well and add the vanilla extract.
7. Mix into a smooth batter.
8. Add the date paste and mix well.
9. In a pan, heat the butter over medium heat.
10. Add the batter using a spoon and fry them golden brown from both sides.
11. Repeat with all the batter.
12. Serve with melted butter on top.

Nutrition:
- Calories: 281 kcal
- Total Fat: 20g
- Carbohydrates: 4.5g
- Protein: 10.5g

#3 Low Carb Pancake Crepes

Preparation Time: 10 minutes
Cooking Time: 10 minutes
Servings: 2
Ingredients:
- 3 ounces cream cheese
- 1 tsp. ground cinnamon
- 1 tbsp. honey
- 1 tsp. ground cardamom
- 1 tsp. butter
- 2 egg, beaten

Directions:
1. In a bowl, whisk the eggs finely.
2. Beat the cream cheese in a different bowl until it becomes soft.
3. Add the egg mixture to the softened cream cheese and mix well until there are no lumps left.
4. Add cinnamon, cardamom, and honey to it. Mix well. The batter would be runnier than of pancake batter.
5. In a pan, add the butter and heat over medium heat.
6. Add the batter using a scooper; that way, all the size of the crepes would be the same.
7. Fry them golden brown on both sides.
8. Repeat the process with the rest of the batter.
9. Drizzle some honey on top and enjoy.

Nutrition:
- Calories: 241 kcal
- Total Fat: 21.8 g
- Carbohydrates: 2.4g
- Protein: 9.6 g

#4 Chia Seed Banana Blueberry Delight

Preparation Time: 30 minutes
Cooking Time: 0 minutes
Servings: 2

Ingredients:
- 1 cup yogurt
- ½ cup blueberries
- 1/2 tsp. Salt
- 1/2 tsp. Cinnamon
- 1 banana
- 1 tsp. Vanilla Extract
- 1/4 cup Chia Seeds

Directions:
1. Discard the skin of the banana.
2. Cut into semi-thick circles.
3. You can mash them or keep them as a whole if you like to bite into your fruits.
4. Clean the blueberries properly and rinse well.
5. Soak the chia seeds in water for 30 minutes or longer.
6. Drain the chia seeds and transfer them into a bowl.
7. Add the yogurt and mix well.
8. Add the salt, cinnamon, and vanilla and mix again.
9. Now fold in the bananas and blueberries gently.
10. If you want to add dried fruit or nuts, add it and then serve immediately.
11. This is best served cold.

Nutrition:
- Calories: 260 kcal
- Total Fat: 26.6g
- Carbohydrates: 17.4g
- Protein: 4.1g

#5 Morning Meatloaf

Preparation Time: 10 minutes
Cooking Time: 20 minutes
Servings: 6
Ingredients:
- 1 ½ pound of breakfast sausage
- 6 large organic eggs
- 2 tbsp. of unsweetened non-dairy milk
- 1 small onion, finely chopped
- 2 medium garlic cloves, peeled and minced
- 4-ounces of cream cheese softened and cubed
- 1 cup of shredded cheddar cheese
- 2 tbsp. of scallions, chopped
- 1 cup of water

Directions:
1. Add all the ingredients apart from water in a large bowl. Stir until well combined.
2. Form the sausage mixture into a meatloaf and wrap with a sheet of aluminum foil. Ensure that the meatloaf fits inside your Instant Pot. If not, remove parts of the mixture and reserve for future use.
3. Once you wrap the meatloaf into a packet, add 1 cup of water and a trivet to your Instant Pot. Put the meatloaf on the trivet's top.
4. Cover and cook for 25 minutes on high pressure. When done, quickly release the pressure. Carefully remove the lid.
5. Unwrap the meatloaf and check if the meatloaf is done. Serve and enjoy!

Nutrition:
- Calories: 592 kcal
- Total Fat: 49.5g
- Carbohydrates: 2.5g
- Protein: 11g

#6 Savory Breakfast Muffins

Preparation Time: 10 minutes
Cooking Time: 35 minutes
Servings: 6

Ingredients:
- 8 eggs
- 1 cup shredded cheese
- Salt and pepper to taste
- ½ tsp. baking powder
- ¼ cup diced onion
- 2/3 cup coconut flour
- 1 ½ cup spinach
- ¼ cup full fat coconut milk
- 1 tbsp. basil, chopped
- ½ cup cooked chicken, diced finely

Directions:
1. Preheat the oven to 375-degree F.
2. Use butter or oil to grease your muffin tray or you can use muffin paper liners.
3. In a large mixing bowl, whisk the eggs.
4. Add in the coconut milk and mix again.
5. Gradually shift in the coconut flour with baking powder salt.
6. Add in the cooked chicken, onion, spinach, basil, and combine well.
7. Add the cheese and mix again.
8. Pour the mixture onto your muffin liners.
9. Bake for about 25 minutes.
10. Serve at room temperature.

Nutrition:
- Calories: 388 kcal
- Total Fat: 25.8g
- Carbohydrates: 8.6g
- Protein: 25.3g

Lunch

#7 Low-Carb All Day Mexican Bowl

Preparation Time: 5 minutes
Cooking Time: 20-25 minutes
Servings: 2

Ingredients:
- 2 mexican chorizo sausages (160g/5.6oz)
- 2 gluten-free Italian style sausages (160g/5.6oz)
- ½ jalapeno pepper (7g/0.3oz)
- 1 tbsp. fresh oregano or 1 tsp dried oregano
- 1 small yellow onion, diced (45g/1.6oz)
- ½ cup halved cherry tomatoes (75g/2.6oz)
- ½ red bell pepper, chopped (60g/2.1oz)
- 1 medium spring onion, sliced (15g/0.5oz)
- 1 tbsp. extra virgin olive oil (15ml)
- ¼ tsp. coconut aminos
- 1 tsp. fresh lime juice
- 1 tbsp. chopped fresh coriander
- 2 large eggs
- ½ large avocado, sliced (100g/3.5oz)
- ¼ tsp. paprika
- salt and pepper, to taste

Optional extras:
- few tortilla chips made from keto tortillas
- dollop of sour cream
- 1-2 tsp. sriracha sauce (you can make your own fermented sriracha)

Directions:
1. Remove the casing from the Italian sausage and chorizo. Fry the meat in a dry, non-stick pan, for 5 minutes breaking it up as you fry so it resembles a mince consistency, until browned.
2. Add the onion, paprika and jalapeño and fry on a medium / low heat for 6–8 minutes until the onion is soft and translucent. Set aside.
3. In a bowl, mix the olive oil, lime, coconut aminos and a pinch of salt and pepper in a bowl. Toss with the tomatoes, oregano, red pepper and spring onion to make a quick salsa.
4. Poach the eggs by filling a saucepan full of boiling water from the kettle. Bring to a light simmer over a medium heat and season with salt.
5. Crack each egg into a cup one at a time. Swirl the water gently with a spoon in a circular direction and carefully pour the egg into the water. Cook for 3 (soft) - 5 minutes (hard). Remove with a slotted spoon and place on kitchen paper to drain.
6. Place the sausage meat in your bowl and top with your poached egg, avocado, sour cream, chopped coriander and sriracha sauce for attitude and optional keto tortilla chips.
7. Best when served fresh, but can be stored in the fridge for 1 day.

Nutrition:
- Calories: 726 kcal
- Total Fat: 60g
- Carbohydrates: 7.9g
- Protein: 32.5g

#8 Speedy Low-Carb Tuna Lunch Bowl

Preparation Time: 5 minutes
Cooking Time: 15 minutes
Servings: 3

Ingredients:
- 1 tuna steak (120g/4.2oz) - or use tinned, drained tuna
- 1 tsp. sesame seeds
- pinch of sea salt
- 1 tsp. ghee, butter or virgin coconut oil
- ½ avocado, sliced (100g/3.5oz)
- 10 pitted black olives (30g/1.1oz)
- 1 tbsp. mayonnaise (15g/0.5oz) - you can make your own mayo
- ½ medium cucumber, sliced (70g/2.5oz)
- 6 quails eggs or 1 large egg
- ¼ small red onion, finely sliced (15g/0.5oz)
- 10 walnut halves (20g/0.7oz)
- 1 tbsp. extra virgin olive oil (15ml)
- large handful of watercress (50g/1.8oz)

Directions:
1. Preheat the oven to 180 °C/ 355 °F (fan assisted) 200 °C/ 400 °F (conventional). Wash and dry the watercress.
2. Place the walnuts on a baking tray and roast in the oven for 6-8 minutes until golden. Remove from the oven and allow to cool.
3. Coat the tuna with sesame seeds, ghee and a pinch of salt. If using tinned tuna, simply sprinkle the sesame seeds over the salad in the end.
4. Heat a griddle pan and fry the tuna to your liking - 1 ½ minutes per side for pink, up to 3 minutes per side for well done. Remove from the heat and allow to cool slightly before slicing.
5. Boil the quail eggs for 2-3 minutes (or about 10 minutes for large eggs). Plunge into cold water before peeling.
6. Slice the rest of ingredients.
7. Place the watercress in a bowl and add olives, halved quail eggs, and avocado, walnuts and drizzle with 1 tbsp of olive oil and top with 1 tbsp of mayonnaise. Optionally, garnish with ground black pepper.
8. It tastes the best when served fresh but can be stored in the fridge for 1 day.

Nutrition:
- Calories: 866 kcal
- Total Fat: 71.3g
- Carbohydrates: 6.4g
- Protein: 44.2g

#9 Smoked Salmon, Avocado & Egg Lunch Bowl

Preparation Time: 10 minutes
Cooking Time: 25 minutes
Servings: 1

Ingredients:

Salad:
- 2 tbsp. pumpkin seeds (16g/0.6oz)
- 1 tsp. sesame seeds
- ½ large avocado (100g/3.5oz)
- 1 tsp. lime or lemon juice
- 1 tsp. extra virgin olive oil
- 1/8 tsp. chile flakes
- pinch of salt and pepper
- 1 small head crispy lettuce such as baby gem (100g/3.5oz)
- 1 large egg
- 150g smoked salmon (5.3oz)

To Serve:
- 2 tbsp. extra virgin olive oil (30ml)
- 1 tbsp. lemon juice (15ml)
- pinch of salt and pepper
- 1 tbsp. butter, ghee or bacon grease (14g/0.5oz)
- 1 tsp. paprika
- 2 tbsp. full-fat greek yogurt or paleo mayonnaise (30g/1.1oz)

Directions:

1. Preheat the oven to 180 °C/ 355 °F (fan assisted) 200 °C/ 400 °F (conventional). Place the seeds on a baking tray and roast for 8 minutes until golden. Remove from the oven and allow to cool. Alternatively, roast on a hot dry pan for a few minutes until the pumpkin seeds puff up.
2. Place the peeled and pitted avocado into a bowl and smash using a fork. Mix all the smashed avocado ingredients together in a small bowl. Add lime juice, olive oil, chile flakes, salt, and pepper, and mix well.
3. In a separate bowl, mix the dressing ingredients together.
4. Poach the eggs by filling a saucepan full of boiling water from the kettle. Bring to a light simmer over a medium heat and season with salt.
5. Crack each egg into a cup one at a time. Swirl the water gently with a spoon in a circular direction, and carefully pour the egg into the water. Cook for about 3 (soft) - 5 minutes (hard). Remove with a slotted spoon and place on kitchen paper to drain. Smoked Salmon, Avocado & Egg Lunch Bawl.
6. Melt the butter in a pan on a low heat. Once melted, add the paprika and immediately turn off the heat. Do not let the butter burn, or it will discolor it. Allow cooling slightly. Place yogurt in a bowl and swirl through paprika butter.
7. Place the baby gem lettuce leaves in your serving bowl.
8. Top with smoked salmon, dressing, toasted seeds, smashed avocado, and chilli flakes and paprika butter yogurt.
9. Top with the poached egg. Tastes best when served fresh but can be stored in the fridge for up to a day.

Nutrition:
- Calories: 949 kcal
- Total Fat: 80.7g
- Carbohydrates: 7.7g
- Protein: 45g

#10 Stir-Fried Pork with Ginger and Soy Sauce

Preparation Time: 30 minutes
Cooking Time: 10-30 minutes
Servings: 2

Ingredients:
- 250g/9oz pork tenderloin, all visible fat removed, cut into chunks
- 1 tsp. cornflour
- 2 tbsp. dark soy sauce
- low-calorie cooking spray
- 150g/5½oz button mushrooms, sliced
- 2 red peppers, deseeded and sliced
- 75g/2½oz mangetout, trimmed
- 15g/½oz fresh root ginger, cut into thin matchsticks
- 1 garlic clove, thinly sliced
- 4 spring onions, cut into short lengths
- freshly ground black pepper

Directions:
1. Season the pork with pepper. Mix the cornflour with two tablespoons of cold water until smooth, then stir in the soy sauce.
2. Spray a large wok, or deep-frying pan, with cooking spray and place over a high heat. Stir-fry the pork for 1-2 minutes, or until lightly browned but not cooked through. Transfer to a plate.
3. Return, the pan to the heat, reduce the heat a little and spray with more oil. Stir-fry the mushrooms and pepper for 2 minutes. Add the mangetout and cook for a minute. Add the ginger, garlic and spring onions and stir-fry for a few seconds.
4. Return the pork to the pan and pour over the soy sauce mixture. Cook for 1-2 minutes, or until the sauce has thickened and the pork is cooked through. Serve immediately.

Nutrition:
- Calories: 952 kcal
- Total Fat: 28.1g
- Carbohydrates: 17.2g
- Protein: 27g

#11 Keto Crispy Ginger Mackerel Lunch Bawl

Preparation Time: 10 minutes
Cooking Time: 40 minutes
Servings: 2
Ingredients:
Marinade:
- 1 tbsp. grated ginger
- 1 tbsp. lemon juice
- 3 tbsp. olive oil
- 1 tbsp. coconut aminos
- Salt and pepper, to taste

Lunch Bowl:
- 2 (8-ounce) boneless mackerel fillets
- 1-ounce almonds
- 1 ½ cups broccoli
- 1 tbsp. butter
- ½ small yellow onion
- 1/3 cup diced red bell pepper
- 2 small sun-dried tomatoes, chopped
- 4 tbsp. mashed avocado

Directions:
1. Preheat the oven to 400 °F. Line a baking tray with parchment paper or foil. Mix together the grated ginger, lemon juice, olive oil, coconut aminos, and some salt and pepper. Rub half of the marinade on the mackerel fillets.
2. Lay the fillets onto the baking tray with the skin side facing up. Roast for 12-15 minutes or until the skin is crispy.
3. Spread the almonds out on a separate baking sheet. Roast for 5-6 minutes or until they brown. Take out of the oven and cool before chopping.
4. Lightly steam the broccoli until it's started to soften but isn't mushy. Roughly chop it up.
5. Preheat a pan over medium heat, then add the butter and allow it to melt. Fry the onions and peppers until they are soft.
6. Add the broccoli and sun-dried tomatoes, then continue cooking until warmed through.
7. Turn off the heat then mix in the rest of the dressing and roasted almonds. Serve with the avocado.

Nutrition:
- Calories: 649 kcal
- Total Fat: 53.4g
- Carbohydrates: 9.2g
- Protein: 28.05g

#12 Italian Style Meatballs with Courgette 'Tagliatelle'

Preparation Time: 30 minutes
Cooking Time: 10-30 minutes
Servings: 2
Ingredients:
For the Meatballs:
- 250g/9oz extra lean beef mince (5% fat or less)
- 1 small onion, very finely chopped
- 1 tsp. dried mixed herbs
- calorie controlled cooking oil spray
- 1 garlic clove, crushed
- 227g/8oz can chopped tomatoes
- 2 heaped tbsp finely shredded fresh basil leaves, plus extra to garnish

For the Courgette 'Tagliatelle':
- 2 medium courgettes, trimmed and deseeded
- sea salt and freshly ground black pepper

Directions:
1. Place the beef, half the onion, half the mixed herbs and a pinch of salt and pepper in a bowl and mix well. Form into 10 small balls.
2. Spray a medium non-stick frying pan with a little oil and cook the meatballs for 5-7 minutes, occasionally turning until browned on all sides. Transfer to a plate.
3. For the sauce, put the remaining onion in the same pan and cook over a low heat for three minutes, stirring. Add the garlic and cook for a few seconds.
4. Stir in the tomatoes, 300ml/10fl oz. water, the remaining mixed herbs, and shredded basil. Bring to the boil, stirring. Return the meatballs to the pan, reduce the heat to a simmer and cook for 20 minutes, stirring occasionally until the sauce is thick and the meatballs are cooked throughout.
5. Meanwhile, half-fill a medium pan with water and bring to the boil. Use a vegetable peeler to peel the courgettes into ribbons. Cook the courgette in the boiling water for one minute then drain.
6. Divide the courgette ribbons between two plates and top with the meatballs and sauce. Garnish with basil leaves.

Nutrition:
- Calories: 219 kcal
- Total Fat: 22.2g
- Carbohydrates: 55.3g
- Protein: 34.1g

Dinner

#13 Creamy Tuscan Garlic Chicken

Preparation Time: 5 minutes
Cooking Time: 20 minutes
Servings: 6

Ingredients:
- 1½ pounds boneless skinless chicken breasts thinly sliced
- 2 tbsp. olive oil
- 1 cup heavy cream
- 1/2 cup chicken broth
- 1 tsp. garlic powder
- 1 tsp. italian seasoning
- 1/2 cup parmesan cheese
- 1 cup spinach chopped
- 1/2 cup sun dried tomatoes

Directions:
1. In a large skillet add olive oil and cook the chicken on medium-high heat for 3-5 minutes on each side or until brown on each side and cooked until no longer pink in center. Remove chicken and set aside on a plate.
2. Add the heavy cream, chicken broth, garlic powder, italian seasoning, and parmesan cheese. Whisk over medium-high heat until it starts to thicken. Add the spinach and sundried tomatoes and let it simmer until the spinach starts to wilt. Add the chicken back to the pan and serve over pasta if desired.

Nutrition:
- Calories: 368 kcal
- Total Fat: 25g
- Carbohydrates: 7g
- Protein: 30g

#14 Turkey and Peppers

Preparation Time: 5 minutes
Cooking Time: 15 minutes
Servings: 4

Ingredients:
- 1 tsp. salt, divided
- 1 pound turkey tenderloin, cut into thin steaks about ¼-inch thick
- 2 tbsp. extra-virgin olive oil, divided
- ½ large sweet onion, sliced
- 1 red bell pepper, cut into strips
- 1 yellow bell pepper, cut into strips
- ½ tsp. italian seasoning
- ¼ tsp. ground black pepper
- 2 tsp. red wine vinegar
- 1 14-ounce can crushed tomatoes, preferably fire-roasted
- chopped fresh parsley and basil for garnish (optional)

Directions:
1. Sprinkle ½ teaspoon salt over turkey. Heat 1 tablespoon oil in a large non-stick skillet over medium-high heat. Add half of the turkey and cook, until browned on the bottom, 1 to 3 minutes. Flip and continue cooking until cooked all the way through, 1 to 2 minutes. Remove the turkey to a plate with a slotted spatula, tent with foil to keep warm. Add the remaining 1 tablespoon oil to the skillet, reduce heat to medium and repeat with the remaining turkey, 1 to 3 minutes per side.
2. Add onion, bell peppers and the remaining ½ teaspoon salt to the skillet, cover and cook, removing lid to stir often, until the onion and peppers are softening and brown in spots, 5 to 7 minutes.
3. Remove lid, increase heat to medium-high, sprinkle with Italian seasoning and pepper and cook, often stirring until the herbs are fragrant, about 30 seconds. Add vinegar, and cook, stirring until almost completely evaporated, about 20 seconds. Add tomatoes and bring to a simmer, stirring often.
4. Add the turkey to the skillet with any accumulated juices from the plate and bring to a simmer. Reduce heat to medium-low and cook, turning in the sauce until the turkey is hot all the way through, 1 to 2 minutes. Serve topped with parsley and basil if using.

Nutrition:
- Calories: 230 kcal
- Total Fat: 8g
- Carbohydrates: 11g
- Protein: 30g

#15 Shredded Chicken Chili

Preparation Time: 10 minutes
Cooking Time: 20 minutes
Servings: 6

Ingredients:
- 4 chicken breasts large, shredded
- 1 tbsp. butter
- ½ onion chopped
- 2 cups chicken broth
- 10 oz diced tomatoes canned, undrained
- 2 oz tomato paste
- 1 tbsp. chili powder
- 1 tbsp. cumin
- 1/2 tbsp. garlic powder
- 1 jalapeno pepper chopped (optional)
- 4 oz Cream cheese
- salt and pepper to taste

Directions:
1. Prepare chicken by boiling chicken breasts in water or broth on stovetop for 10-12 minutes, just barely covered in liquid. Once the meat is no longer pink, remove from fluid and shred with two forks. This same technique can also be used with a pressure cooker at pressure for 5 minutes with a natural release, or a slow cooker for 4-6 hours. Whatever's clever for you! Rotisserie chicken meat can be substituted for the breasts as well.
2. In a large stockpot, melt the butter over medium-high heat. Add the onion and cook until translucent.
3. Add the shredded chicken, chicken broth, diced tomatoes, tomato paste, chili powder, cumin, garlic powder, and jalapeno to the pot and combine by gently stirring over the burner. Bring to a boil, then drop it down to a simmer over medium-low heat and cover for 10 minutes.
4. Cut cream cheese into small, 1-inch chunks.
5. Remove lid and mix in the cream cheese. Increase the heat back up to medium-high and continue to stir until the cream cheese is completely blended in. Remove from heat and season with salt and pepper to taste.
6. Eat as-is or garnish with toppings of your choice.

Nutrition:
- Calories: 201 kcal
- Total Fat: 11g
- Carbohydrates: 7g
- Protein: 18g

#16 Taco Stuffed Avocados

Preparation Time: 15 minutes
Cooking Time: 5 minutes
Servings: 6

Ingredients:
- 1 pound ground beef
- 1 tbsp. chili powder
- ½ tsp. salt
- ¾ tsp. cumin
- ½ tsp. dried oregano
- ¼ tsp. garlic powder
- ¼ tsp. onion powder
- 4 ounces tomato sauce
- 3 avocados halved
- 1 cup shredded cheddar cheese
- ¼ cup cherry tomatoes sliced
- ¼ cup lettuce shredded

Additional Toppings:
- cilantro
- sour cream

Directions:
1. Add the ground beef to a medium size sauce pan. Cook over medium heat until browned.
2. Drain the grease and add the seasonings and the tomato sauce. Stir to combine. Cook for about 3-4 minutes.
3. Remove the pit from the halved avocados. Load the crater left from the pit with the taco meat. Top with cheese, tomatoes, lettuce, cilantro and sour cream.
4. If you want to make a larger area in the avocado for the toppings, spoon out some of the avocado and set aside to make guacamole! Then fill with toppings.

Nutrition:
- Calories: 410 kcal
- Total Fat: 16g
- Carbohydrates: 5g
- Protein: 26g

#17 Asparagus Stuffed Chicken

Preparation Time: 10 minutes
Cooking Time: 20 minutes
Servings: 3

Ingredients:
- 3 chicken breasts
- 1 tsp. garlic paste
- 12 stalks asparagus (stalks removed)
- 1/2 cup cream cheese
- 1 tbsp. butter
- 1 tsp. olive oil
- 3/4 cup marinara sauce
- 1 cup shredded mozzarella
- salt and pepper to taste

Directions:
1. To start prepping the chicken, butterfly the chicken (or slice it in half without slicing it all the way through. The chicken breast should open out like a butterfly with one end still intact in the middle). Remove the hardy stalks of the asparagus and set aside.
2. Rub salt, pepper and garlic paste all over the chicken breasts (inside and outside). Divide cream cheese between the chicken breasts and spread it on the inside. Place four stalks of asparagus and then fold one side of the breast over the other, tucking it in place with a toothpick to make sure it doesn't come open.
3. Preheat the oven, and set it to broiler. Add butter and olive oil to a hot skillet and place the chicken breasts in it. Cook the breasts on each side for 6-7 minutes (total time will be 14-15 minutes depending on the size of the breast) till the chicken is almost cooked through.
4. Top each breast with 1/4 cup marinara sauce, and divide the shredded mozzarella on top. Place in the oven and broil for 5 minutes till the cheese melts.

Nutrition:
- Calories: 317 kcal
- Total Fat: 20.6g
- Carbohydrates: 11.2g
- Protein: 23.1g

#18 Ground Beef & Cabbage Stir Fry
Preparation Time: 5 minutes
Cooking Time: 20 minutes
Servings: 3
Ingredients:
- 1 pound ground beef (I typically use 85% lean)
- 1 (9-ounce) bag coleslaw (or 5 cups mix of shredded fresh cabbage and sliced carrots)
- 2 scallions (also known as green onions), thinly sliced
- 1 tbsp. peeled freshly grated ginger
- 2 tbsp. soy sauce (both regular and low-sodium varieties work well; I use the brand Kikkoman)
- 1 tbsp. sriracha sauce (you can use the brand Huy Fong; can substitute with another chili garlic sauce or your favorite hot sauce)
- (optional) black sesame seeds

Directions:
1. Stir soy sauce and sriracha together with a spoon in a small mixing bowl until smooth; set aside.
2. Prepare a pan large enough to simultaneously hold ground beef and coleslaw; I use a nonstick 10-inch pan with 3-inch-tall sides. No lid needed. It's not necessary to pre-heat the pan, and oil is not required.
3. Add ground beef to the pan over medium-high heat; cook until browned and crumbled, breaking up the meat with a stiff utensil, about 5 minutes. Do not drain fat, which will be used to fry coleslaw in the next step.
4. Keeping beef in the pan, stir in coleslaw mix. Cook until cabbage is wilted and tender, stirring frequently, about 5 minutes.
5. Reduce heat to medium-low. Stir in prepared sauce (soy sauce and sriracha) and ginger until well-mixed, about 1 minute.
6. Turn off the heat. Stir in sliced scallions, and optionally garnish with sesame seeds. Serve while hot.
7. Leftovers: Cover and store leftovers in the refrigerator for up to a few days. Reheat using the microwave or on the stovetop until warmed through.

Nutrition:
- Calories: 420 kcal
- Total Fat: 22g
- Carbohydrates: 6g
- Protein: 39g

Snacks

#19 Low-Carb Brownies

Preparation Time: 10 minutes
Cooking Time: 20 minutes
Servings: 16

Ingredients:
- 7 tbsp. coconut oil, melted
- 6 tbsp. plant-based sweetener
- 1 large egg
- 2 egg yolk
- 1/2 tsp. mint extract
- 5 ounces sugar-free dark chocolate
- ¼ cup plant-based chocolate protein powder
- 1 tsp. baking soda
- ¼ tsp. Sea salt
- 2 tbsp. vanilla almond milk, unsweetened

Directions:
1. Start by preheating the oven to 350°F and then take an 8x8 inch pan and line it with parchment paper, being sure to leave some extra sticking up to use later to help you get them out of the pan after they are cooked.
2. Into a medium-sized vessel, use a hand mixer, and blend 5 Tablespoons of the coconut oil (save the rest for later), as well as the egg, Erythritol, egg yolks, and the mint extract all together for 1 minute. After this minute, the mixture will become a lighter yellow hue.
3. Take 4 oz. of the chocolate and put it in a (microwave-safe) bowl, as well as with the other 2 Tablespoons of melted coconut oil.
4. Cook this chocolate and oil mixture on half power, at 30-second intervals, being sure to stir at each interval, just until the chocolate becomes melted and smooth
5. While the egg mixture is being beaten, add in the melted chocolate mixture into the egg mixture until this becomes thick and homogenous.
6. Add in your protein powder of choice, salt, baking soda, and stir until homogenous. Then, vigorously whisk your almond milk in until the batter becomes a bit smoother.
7. Finely chop the rest of your chocolate and stir these bits of chocolate into the batter you have made.
8. Spread the batter evenly into the pan you have prepared, and bake this until the edges of the batter just begin to become darker, and the center of the batter rises a little bit. You can also tell by sliding a toothpick into the middle, and when it comes out clean, it is ready. This will take approximately 20 to 21 minutes. Be sure that you do NOT over bake them!
9. Let them cool in the pan they cooked in for about 20 minutes. Then, carefully use the excess paper handles to take the brownies out of the pan and put them onto a wire cooling rack.
10. Make sure that they cool completely, and when they do, cut them, and they are ready to eat!

Nutrition:
- Calories: 107 kcal
- Total Fat: 10g
- Carbohydrates: 5.7g
- Protein: 2.5g

#20 Apple Bread

Preparation Time: 10 minutes
Cooking Time: 20 minutes
Servings: 10

Ingredients:
- ½ cup honey
- ½ tsp. nutmeg
- ½ tsp. salt
- 1 cup applesauce, sweetened
- 1 tsp. baking soda
- 1 tsp. vanilla extract
- 2 ¼ cup whole wheat flour
- 2 large eggs
- 2 tbsp. vegetable oil
- 2 tsp. baking powder
- 2 tsp. cinnamon
- 4 cup apples, diced

Directions:
1. Preheat oven to 375° Fahrenheit and oil a loaf pan with non-stick spray or your choice of oil.
2. Beat eggs in a mixing bowl and stir until completely smooth.
3. Add the honey, oil, applesauce, cinnamon, vanilla, nutmeg, baking powder, baking soda, and salt. Whisk until completely combined and smooth.
4. Add the flour into the bowl and whisk to combine, making sure not to over-mix. Simply stir it enough to incorporate the flour.
5. Add apples to the batter and mix once more to combine.
6. Pour the batter into the loaf pan and smooth the top with your spatula.
7. Bake for 60 minutes or until an inserted toothpick in the center comes out clean.
8. Let stand for 10 minutes, then transfer the loaf to a cooling rack to cool completely.
9. Slice into 10 pieces and serve!

Nutrition:
- Calories: 210 kcal
- Total Fat: 5g
- Carbohydrates: 41g
- Protein: 5g

#21 Coconut Protein Balls

Preparation Time: 20 minutes
Cooking Time: 0 minutes
Servings: 27

Ingredients:
- ¼ cup dark chocolate chips
- ½ cup coconut flakes, unsweetened
- ½ cup of water
- 1 ½ cup almonds, raw & unsalted
- 2 tbsp. cocoa powder, unsweetened
- 3 cup medjool dates, pitted
- 4 scoops whey protein powder, unsweetened

Directions:
1. Blend almonds in a food processor until a flour is formed. Add the water and dates to the flour and continue to process until fully combined. You may need to stop intermittently to scrape down the sides of the bowl.
2. Add cocoa and protein to the processor and continue to process until well combined. You may need to stop intermittently to scrape down the sides of the bowl.
3. Pull the blade out of the processor (carefully!) and use your spatula to gather all of the dough in one place inside the processor container.
4. On a plate or in a large, shallow dish, spread the coconut flakes.
5. Scoop out a little bit of the dough at a time using a spoon, and roll it into balls, then roll each one in the coconut flakes.
6. Refrigerate for at least 30 min before enjoying.

Nutrition:
- Calories: 108 kcal
- Total Fat: 4g
- Carbohydrates: 16g
- Protein: 5g

#22 Protein Bars

Preparation Time: 10 minutes
Cooking Time: 30 minutes
Servings: 12
Ingredients:
For the Bars:
- 1/3 cup coconut oil
- 1/3 cup creamy peanut butter, unsalted
- 1/3 cup almond meal
- ½ cup milk of your choice, unsweetened
- 1 ½ cup of protein powder

For the Topping:
- 2 tbsp. chocolate chips
- 1 tbsp. coconut oil
- 3 tbsp. almonds, chopped

Directions:
1. In a microwave-safe bowl, combine peanut butter, milk and all but one tablespoon of the coconut oil. Heat for 30-second intervals, stirring in between, until completely smooth.
2. Mix almond meal and protein powder into the bowl and combine well until a crumbly dough is combined.
3. Line a baking dish with a parchment paper and flatten the dough into it until an even layer is formed.
4. In a small, microwave-safe bowl, put the chocolate chips and 1 tbsp. of coconut oil and heat for 30-second intervals, while stirring in between until completely smooth.
5. Pour the mixture of chocolate over the bars and spread it evenly. Sprinkle the almonds on top and then freeze the bars for about 20 minutes, or refrigerate them for about an hour.
6. Cut into 12 evenly-shaped bars and enjoy!

Nutrition:
- Calories: 186 kcal
- Total Fat: 14g
- Carbohydrates: 7g
- Protein: 8g

#23 Blueberry Muffins

Preparation Time: 5 minutes
Cooking Time: 25 minutes
Servings: 12

Ingredients:
- ½ tsp. baking soda
- ¼ cup of vegetable oil
- ¼ tsp. salt
- 1 ½ cup blueberries, frozen
- 1 cup applesauce, unsweetened
- 1 tsp. vanilla extract
- 1/3 cup honey
- 2 cup whole wheat flour
- 1 tsp. cinnamon
- 2 large eggs, beaten
- 2 tsp. baking powder

Directions:
1. Preheat oven to 350° Fahrenheit and line a muffin tin with paper liners.
2. Combine eggs, apple sauce, honey, oil, vanilla extract, cinnamon, baking soda, salt, and baking powder in a bowl. Whisk until completely combined, ensuring that there are no lumps of baking powder or soda.
3. Add flour to the batter and whisk until just combined.
4. Add blueberries and mix.
5. Fill the muffin tins and bake for 22-25 minutes or until a toothpick inserted into the middle of the middlemost muffin becomes clean.
6. Let cool for 30 minutes before transferring to a cooling rack to cool completely. Serve and enjoy!

Nutrition:
- Calories: 329 kcal
- Total Fat: 14g
- Carbohydrates: 40g
- Protein: 14g

#24 Southwest Chicken Salad

Preparation Time: 15 minutes
Cooking time: 15 minutes
Servings: 8

Ingredients:
- ¼ cup extra virgin olive oil
- ¼ cup red onion, finely chopped
- 1 cup corn, drained
- 1 can low-sodium black beans, rinsed & drained
- 1 jalapeño, seeded & minced
- 1 tsp. chili powder
- 1 tsp. cumin
- 1 tsp. garlic powder
- 1 tsp. onion powder
- 2 bell peppers, diced
- 2 lb. limes, juiced
- 2 lb. chicken thighs, cooked and diced
- 2 tbsp. cilantro, finely chopped
- 3 cup quinoa, cooked
- sea salt & black pepper, to taste

Directions:
1. In a small bowl, mix chili powder, lime juice, onion powder, garlic powder, cumin, and cilantro. Mix thoroughly and set aside.
2. In a large mixing bowl, combine all other ingredients and toss until thoroughly combined.
3. Drizzle seasoning mixture over the salad and toss to coat completely.
4. Cover and refrigerate for 30 minutes before serving.

Nutrition:
- Calories: 217 kcal
- Total Fat: 9g
- Carbohydrates: 30g
- Protein: 7g

www.ingramcontent.com/pod-product-compliance
Lightning Source LLC
Chambersburg PA
CBHW080023110526
44587CB00021BA/3744